Praise

'Business growth is downstream from lead generation. If you can't generate leads, almost nothing else matters. This book is going to get you drowning in leads.'
— **Daniel Priestley**, founder, ScoreApp.com, and bestselling author of *Key Person of Influence*

'Francis Rodino's *Leads Machine* is a must-read for any local business owner or entrepreneur looking to revolutionise lead generation. This book is packed with cutting-edge strategies that blend automation, AI and a proven, predictable system to attract quality leads effortlessly. Francis has created a step-by-step guide that not only demystifies scaling to eight figures but also empowers service-based businesses to unlock sustainable growth. If you're ready to take your business to the next level with a scalable, automated approach, *Leads Machine* is your blueprint to success.'
— **Shaun Clark**, co-founder, HighLevel

'In *Leads Machine*, Francis Rodino breaks down the complexities of lead generation into a simple, actionable system. The RED method is a fantastic tool for service businesses.'
— **Alison Warner**, founder, Evolve and Grow Coaching

'Francis Rodino's RED method offers a clear, step-by-step process for consistently generating quality leads. It's a must-have strategy for any business looking to scale to new heights.'
— **Sebastian Bates**, founder, Warrior Academy and Bates Foundation

'As a healthcare practitioner, I know the struggle of building and growing a patient base. *Leads Machine* shows you how to automate the marketing process so you can focus on patient care and practice growth without constantly chasing new leads.'
— **Alex Smilanic**, founder, Wellbeing Revolution Training

'Franchisees and service businesses must take leads seriously. The RED method is great for growth, but Francis goes beyond that – teaching you how to turn those leads into profits.'
— **Rune Sovndahl**, author and co-founder, Fantastic Services

'If generating consistent leads for your service business has been a challenge, Francis Rodino's RED method is the solution you've been waiting for. This nine-step methodology is a game changer, providing a clear, actionable path to scaling your business to six or seven figures. RED makes it simple to build a predictable, effective and continuous lead-generation system.'
— **Mathieu Gorge**, founder and CEO, VigiTrust

'This book reveals the power of automation and how to integrate it into your business for maximum impact. It's a game changer for entrepreneurs ready to build efficient, scalable systems.'
— **Gary Das**, bestselling author and founder, Leads to Lifestyle

'Tired of wondering where your next client will come from? *Leads Machine* offers small businesses a proven, automated system that delivers consistent, high-quality leads. It's the go-to guide for businesses ready to level up with ads.'
— **Jo Wood and Zoe Whitman**, hosts of *The Bookkeepers' Podcast*

'If lead generation feels like a mystery, *Leads Machine* will change that. Francis Rodino provides a step-by-step approach to creating a reliable, automated system for attracting quality clients.'
— **Freddie Pullen**, agency owner and host of *The Healthy Entrepreneur Podcast*

'In a competitive recruitment market, positioning your brand is crucial. *Leads Machine* outlines how to create an automated lead generation system that keeps your business visible while you focus on delivering quality.'
— **Alan Furley**, co-founder and CEO, ISL Talent

'For service business owners looking to scale efficiently, *Leads Machine* is a must-read. Francis equips you with the strategies and tools to generate consistent leads and achieve predictable results.'
  — **Paul McGillivray**, co-founder and CTO, Remote.Online, and author of *Scope to Scale*

'Growing an SaaS company is tough when lead generation is inconsistent, but *Leads Machine* offers a solution. Francis Rodino gives you the tools to automate the process, target the right audience and convert leads into loyal customers.'
  — **Lee Russel**, author of *The Minimal Viable Launch*

LEADS MACHINE

THE NINE-STEP SYSTEM TO GENERATE CONSISTENT, PREDICTABLE SALES AND SCALE YOUR SERVICE BUSINESS

FRANCIS RODINO

Re think

First published in Great Britain in 2025
by Rethink Press (www.rethinkpress.com)

© Copyright Francis Rodino

All rights reserved. No part of this publication may be reproduced, stored in or introduced into a retrieval system, or transmitted, in any form, or by any means (electronic, mechanical, photocopying, recording or otherwise) without the prior written permission of the publisher.

The right of Francis Rodino to be identified as the author of this work has been asserted by him in accordance with the Copyright, Designs and Patents Act 1988.

This book is sold subject to the condition that it shall not, by way of trade or otherwise, be lent, resold, hired out, or otherwise circulated without the publisher's prior consent in any form of binding or cover other than that in which it is published and without a similar condition including this condition being imposed on the subsequent purchaser.

Cover image licensed by Ingram Image

To all the determined, courageous small business owners out there who've taken the leap into entrepreneurship, this book is for you. To everyone embarking on this journey of growth and innovation, here's to the exciting road ahead and the countless success stories yet to be written.

Contents

Foreword by Daniel Priestley — 1

Introduction: Your Blueprint to Consistent, Predictable Sales — 3
    The RED Method — 6
    Why listen to me? — 8

PART ONE   Mindset Mastery — 13

  1 Adopting The Winning Mindset — 17
    Avoiding the trap of 'hope marketing' — 20
    The Revenue Growth Formula — 22

  2 Future-Proof Your Business — 27
    Where are you now? — 29
    Business in the Fourth Industrial Revolution — 35
    From technician to business owner — 41
    Why your marketing doesn't work — 44
    Data is the new gold — 47

3 The RED Method: The Nine Steps To Unlocking Consistent Predictable Sales	**51**
Three levers to grow your business	53
Overview of the RED Method accelerators	55
PART TWO Your Marketing Roadmap: From Confusion To Clarity	**63**
4 Accelerator 1: Market – Master Your Market To Become The Go-To Authority	**69**
Defining your ideal customer	73
Knowing your competitors	80
Building your market visibility	85
5 Accelerator 2: Message – Craft Irresistible Messaging That Converts Customers Into Action	**97**
Craft the perfect pitch	101
Building your value stack	105
Why you need a 'unique mechanism'	114
How to craft irresistible offer 'hooks'	118
6 Accelerator 3: Map – Design A Customer Journey That Builds Trust And Drives Sales	**123**
The automation advantage	124
The 3% Rule: Understanding buyer segments	127
The six stages of the sales funnel	132

PART THREE The Engine: From Antiquated To Automated — **151**

7 Accelerator 4: Capture – Hook Your Ideal Clients With Irresistible Bait — **157**

   The smart way to capture leads — 160

   Your CRM: Stay organised, stay connected, stay automated — 170

   Lead management — 172

   Personalised marketing — 174

8 Accelerator 5: Cultivate – Nurture Relationships for Lifelong Wins — **177**

   Your competitive edge: Speed to lead — 179

   Your 'Zero Moment of Truth' — 181

   Lead nurture stages — 183

   The power of digital assets — 189

9 Accelerator 6: Convert – Build An Autopilot System To Close Sales — **193**

   Personalised follow-ups that close the deal — 195

   Calls to action — 196

   Urgency and scarcity: The psychology of action — 198

   Seamless buying experiences — 200

   Metrics matter: Measure what drives success — 202

The sales pipeline: Track, manage, convert	205
Automation and AI: Your 24/7 sales team	210

PART FOUR Drive: From Invisible To Irresistible — 213

10 Accelerator 7: Reach – Reach More People, Make A Bigger Impact — 221

Using Google and Facebook Ads to scale your business	225
Breaking the scroll: How disruptive advertising works	226
Understanding campaign types	228
Intent-driven advertising – the power of Google Ads	237
Retargeting ads: Turning lost opportunities into sales	245
The nine commandments of digital advertising success	249

11 Accelerator 8: Resell – Turn Customers Into Raving Fans And Repeat Buyers — 261

Selling more to existing customers	263
Maximising ROI with a value ladder	265
Loyalty pays: Building a base of repeat customers	269
Building recurring revenue through subscriptions	272

Beyond the sale: Turning clients into raving fans	276
The road ahead	280

12 Accelerator 9: Refine – Optimise Your Marketing For Lasting Success — 283

Ad Optimisation Cheat Sheet	287
Optimising your metrics for maximum ROI	294
Split and A/B testing: Find what works best	301

Conclusion: Your Business Future – Drift Or Decide — 305

Acknowledgements — 311

The Author — 313

Foreword

by Daniel Priestley

In the world of business, everything flows downstream from one activity: lead generation. If you can't grab attention and spark interest, the brilliance of your offer becomes irrelevant. A steady stream of leads is the lifeblood of most companies – without warm leads, sales stop, top talent walks away and growth grinds to a halt. This is why lead generation isn't just a piece of the puzzle; it's the first domino that sets off a chain reaction of business growth.

As the founder of ScoreApp.com, I've been able to see first-hand countless stories of businesses that transform and grow just by getting their lead generation sorted. It's incredible how things shift when you stop chasing clients and instead create a system that attracts them.

Francis Rodino gets it. He understands that whether you're looking for new customers, team members, investors or partners, it all starts with a lead – a person who raises their hand and says, 'I'm interested.' But generating warm leads is both an art and a science. Today, it's no longer just about collecting contact details; it's about engaging people by grabbing their attention, educating and entertaining them, and inspiring them to take that all-important first step.

In *Leads Machine*, Francis breaks down how to manufacture demand in a world drowning in choices. The industrial age was about reliable, systematic production of goods, but today, success lies in distribution – getting your offer in front of the right people at the right time, with the right message.

This book is more than just a guide; it's a playbook for entrepreneurs and business leaders who want to master the art of lead generation and build sustainable, scalable success.

Daniel Priestley
Founder, ScoreApp.com

Introduction: Your Blueprint to Consistent, Predictable Sales

Just imagine… a new reality where customers are knocking on your door every single day. Your business, *oversubscribed*. You can pick and choose who to work with, and you have a waiting list of enthusiastic clients itching to spend their money with you. Your five-star reputation precedes you, and you are respected as an authority in your space. You have time to focus on growing your business, doing what you love and delivering outstanding services to your customers. Your business is the veritable first choice in your marketplace.

In this world, these are the kinds of things that happen:

- When people search on Google, they find you first.

- When they pit you against the competition, they choose you *every time*.

- They find your brand everywhere when they're looking for help.

- They see your amazing testimonials and trustworthy track record.

- Even when they're not yet ready to buy, you'll be there when they are.

- When they jump on a discovery, demo or consultation call with you, they are primed and ready to buy.

- They could go elsewhere if they wanted to, but they have no desire to work with anyone but you.

That's the dream, right – consistent, predictable sales?

That's why you started a business, because you had the ambition to achieve more, earn more, make a greater impact for your clients, family and community. And this is something to celebrate. The very fact that you're still in business, reading a book about scaling with automated sales funnels, is an achievement you should be proud of.

According to the US Bureau of Labor Statistics (BLS), 50% of businesses fail within the first five years and 65% fail within the first ten years.[1] So if you're

---

1 MT Deane, 'Top 6 reasons new businesses fail', *Investopedia* (1 June 2024), www.investopedia.com/financial-edge/1010/top-6-reasons-new-businesses-fail.aspx, accessed 11 November 2024

INTRODUCTION

keeping the show on the road, that's impressive. But just because things have been going great through word of mouth, good reviews, referrals and so on, there's no guarantee that your lucky streak will last forever. Remember, complacency can trap you.

So why is it so difficult for many business owners to scale, despite their best efforts? They find themselves stressed and burnt out, struggling with stagnant turnover, lack of systems, recruiting challenges and cash flow limitations, and feeling invisible in their market. The core reason is that they lack a predictable selling system – the critical component needed to break through to the next level.

The top 1% of businesses usually share one key trait: an automated sales funnel that consistently attracts, nurtures and converts leads into customers on autopilot. This 'secret weapon' enables them to overcome growth plateaus and scale to seven figures and beyond.

An optimised sales funnel works twenty-four-seven in the background, attracting a steady flow of qualified leads, nurturing them with targeted content and converting them into paying customers without manual effort. This frees up the business owner to focus on serving clients and optimising other areas, instead of constantly chasing sales. It's the ultimate solution to overwhelm and burnout.

In the following chapters, we'll dive into exactly how to construct an automated sales funnel that can take your business to the next level. We'll cover the essential components of a high-converting funnel, strategies to attract your ideal buyers on autopilot, proven tactics to optimise your funnel's performance, common mistakes to avoid and much more.

The RED Method

My proven framework for success and scaling service businesses is built on three critical business levers – Roadmap, Engine and Drive – and nine powerful accelerators. Together, these form the RED Method, an easy-to-follow sales funnel guide in which I've wrapped up twenty years of digital marketing strategy.

The four parts of this book will, in turn, lay the foundations for your future success by instilling the right mindset and getting you up to speed on what the new business landscape looks like and what it offers in the digital world, and then walking you through the three levers for success – Roadmap, Engine and Drive – with their corresponding accelerators, so that you have all the tools you need to grow and scale.

When you put these ideas and tools together and implement the RED Method, you will see three key outcomes for your business:

1. Standout Visibility

2. Greater Control

3. Predictable Sales

INTRODUCTION

These are the outcomes of a predictable, automated system that generates leads, attracts your ideal clients and converts prospects into lucrative clients in a way that's steady, predictable and, most importantly, easily duplicated.

If you're thinking, 'But Francis, this won't work for my business…', you may believe your industry is special. Perhaps it's B2B, or you're dealing with more 'sophisticated' clients, a long sales cycle, or traditional services requiring in-person interactions, like meetings, lunches, networking events or numerous coffees. However, every business, regardless of industry, niche or sales cycle, can benefit from an automated sales funnel.

This is why I created The RED Method: an end-to-end marketing and sales blueprint that is proven to work in competitive markets, and uses timeless marketing strategies coupled with advanced technology. I developed this system primarily for established entrepreneurs, founders and service business owners who are ready to finally break through a sales plateau and scale their businesses with automated marketing and sales systems.

The principles in this book will show you how to bring stability, predictability and certainty to your sales on any scale. You will never have to wonder when or where your next customer is coming from.

How's that for a promise?

I am a pragmatist. I've been in business long enough not to trust tricks, hacks or silver bullets. The RED Method is not a 'magic pill' that will transform your business overnight. It's not focused on saving struggling businesses that are lacking the core fundamentals. The RED Method is a megaphone. It will take what's already working in your business and amplify it so more people have the opportunity to buy from you.

My aim is to help you achieve confidence, calm and clarity around your marketing strategy and help you develop a clear pathway to achieve your business growth goals. I know it can feel confusing thinking about what to do next, and you might have been burnt before, but I promise if you follow the advice in this book, you will be light years ahead of 90% of your competitors.

The RED Method is all about producing consistent, sustainable growth that future-proofs your business for the long term. Even if you're at the top of your game, complacency can trap you. You can still be superseded by a hungry competitor who advertises more effectively and is determined to gain market share. The irony (and sad thing) is you really don't have to be the best at what you do; it's the most visible player in the market who will typically be the most successful.

Why listen to me?

Over the past two decades, I have earned my stripes running multimillion-dollar campaigns for some of the world's biggest and most-loved brands. I then

INTRODUCTION

became an entrepreneur and business owner myself once I realised my digital marketing skills could make a bigger impact on independent, entrepreneur-led businesses.

I currently run two industry-leading automation agencies helping businesses claim back their time and maximise the ROI from their advertising spend. Over the past few years I've helped literally thousands of businesses via coaching, consulting, supplying AI-marketing software and presenting online courses and events. I have saved clients hundreds of thousands of hours of repetitive admin, helped them win market share, beat specific competitors and double or triple their revenue. I've also helped clients cut their working hours and prepare their businesses for sale. I've applied the same logic and system in each case.

I was there right at the beginning of it all, from the dot.com boom (I'm really not that old) through to the advent of AI, overseeing the intersection between new forms of online marketing and new consumer behaviours as they developed. There were huge successes and accomplishments, but there were plenty of failures on the way too. I won't go into detail about them here to avoid embarrassing the guilty parties (mainly myself!), but this phase of my career was defined by experimentation. A few bumps, scrapes and wrong turns were to be expected. As we will see, in every digital marketing success story, there is a degree of testing and optimisation – which is absolutely normal – so factor that in.

My twenty-plus years in digital marketing have taught me that creating marketing that 'works' is rarely a game of chance. There were, and remain, common denominators in marketing that succeeds (and that doesn't). Far from a random activity, there are clear lessons, of various types, shapes and forms, to learn that you can apply to replicate (and scale) success. Success leaves clues. The businesses that were crushing it with their marketing, successfully raising the visibility of their brands, bringing in streams of quality leads, reaching customers consistently and bringing in big money were all doing the same things and, vitally, I realised you could quickly become famous in your marketplace by modelling what works.

My RED Method has been designed, however, with more tangible (and lucrative) benefits in mind than simply becoming famous. It's tried and tested, proven with thousands of businesses across the globe and it's been honed down to a precise step-by-step process. The concepts that inform this book have been used to skyrocket the visibility of big brands, give global organisations marketing control and, over the years, generate millions upon millions in revenue.

Not too shabby, right?

As we navigate an AI-driven future, I hope this book serves as a valuable resource for harnessing the powerful combination of marketing, psychology and technology. May it equip you to anticipate future threats, seize opportunities and make a meaningful impact in your industry and community.

INTRODUCTION

Are you prepared to embark on this journey towards consistent, predictable sales, and transform your business into a powerhouse of efficiency and scale?

The path to extraordinary success begins with a single, intentional step. With the RED Method as your guide, you're poised to make that step count. Let's go!

Alongside reading what follows, you can find free bonus content at www.francisrodino.com/tools.

PART ONE
MINDSET MASTERY

You can apply the RED Method in your business and realise all your entrepreneurial dreams. But to make a start you need to get a few things done right, in the right order. In particular, some deep thinking, some smart work and a plan.

Before getting into the nuts and bolts, we need to lay some solid foundations in terms of mindset, attitude and understanding the business environment that service business owners are operating in today. We need to briefly look back to when you started your business and consider how things have changed in the time since then, whether that's months, years or decades. Your sales processes possibly relied heavily on a combination of ad-hoc spreadsheets, Post-it notes and a good (or not so good) memory. Be honest, in the beginning you thought, 'We'll get clients through word of mouth,' and, 'Customers will come back to us if we do a good enough job.' But you've since found out you only get so far with referrals, right?

You might have already tried some digital marketing but with a mixed bag of results. Do you still feel invisible, despite everything you've tried? I know how it feels to spend money on marketing and not get the results you hoped for because this happened in my business too. Don't worry. Everyone feels burnt out when sales and marketing don't work. I know how painful it is to work hard, invest a lot, try different avenues to bring consistency to your business, yet nothing seems to work.

Alas, it takes trial and error and a lot of testing (not to mention budget) to crack the predictable selling system code. But trust me, when you do, it's like magic!

CASE STUDY: AI-powered marketing – how Warrior Academy boosted sales by 20% in two months

Want to see how embracing cutting-edge tech can supercharge a business? Look no further than our client Warrior Academy. They were already standing out as the UAE's largest martial arts academy for kids, but their recent growth spurt was thanks to some seriously smart marketing moves and a willingness to move with the times.

We helped Warrior Academy implement a game-changing combination of AI chatbots, an advanced CRM and a slick messaging system across WhatsApp,

Facebook and Instagram. The result? A whopping 20% increase in sales in just two months. That's the power of modern marketing tech in action.

Here's how it works: the AI chatbots engage potential customers twenty-four-seven, answering questions and capturing leads. The CRM keeps track of every interaction, ensuring no opportunity slips through the cracks. And the messaging system? It keeps the conversation going across multiple platforms, meeting parents and kids where they already are.

This digital ecosystem doesn't just capture leads – it nurtures them. It sends the right message to the right person at the right time, whether that's a curious first-time visitor or a long-time student considering re-enrolment.

The beauty of this system is its seamless integration. Every part works together to create a smooth journey from initial interest to signed-up student. And once it's set up, it runs like a well-oiled machine, freeing up Warrior Academy's team to focus on what they do best – teaching martial arts and developing character.

Warrior Academy's success shows the massive impact these tools can have. They're not just growing – they're setting new standards in their industry. It's a powerful example of how the right tech, applied strategically, can transform a business's marketing and drive real, measurable growth.

There comes a point when you have to reset your marketing mindset – like Warrior Academy did – if you want to break through to a higher level of success.

In today's rapidly changing technology-enabled marketplace, I know that can feel like a daunting, bewilderingly complex challenge. Not anymore. Automated sales, and all the rewards that come with them, are within your grasp right now.

1
Adopting The Winning Mindset

'If I only had more leads...' I hear business owners cry. When you believe the myth that more leads are the answer to all your marketing and sales problems, you're barely scratching the surface. If we step back and have a think about how we build systems that produce consistent, predictable sales, it can look a little bit like an iceberg. The people who are always chasing 'more leads' and the latest lead generation service are only looking at the tip of the iceberg. That's only about 10% of the whole... The real power of the iceberg is hiding below the surface, at the base.

Think about it – no matter how hard the wind blows at the top or which way it's pushing, that massive iceberg is going to drift wherever its base takes it. That could be in the complete opposite direction of the wind up above, it doesn't make a difference.

It's the same deal in business. All that lead generation and surface-level stuff? They're just the tip. What really counts is the foundation you've built under the surface: your marketing strategies, your systems, your technology. That's what's going to move your business forward, no matter what is happening on the surface. We need to be asking: Where's the real value in your business? What forces are pushing and pulling on that iceberg underneath the waterline?

You see, just below the surface, you've got something less tangible to talk about – results. Everyone talks about wanting results, but these aren't always as clear-cut as a list of leads (of varying quality) in your inbox.

This stuff below the surface? It's where the magic happens. It's messier, sure, and sometimes harder to measure, but it's what really drives your business forward. While everyone else is splashing around in the shallows chasing leads, the smart money is found by diving deep, focusing on building that solid foundation and delivering real, tangible results.

From the perspective of building an effective automated sales funnel, the results that really matter are:

1. Standout Visibility

2. Greater Control

3. Predictable Sales

ADOPTING THE WINNING MINDSET

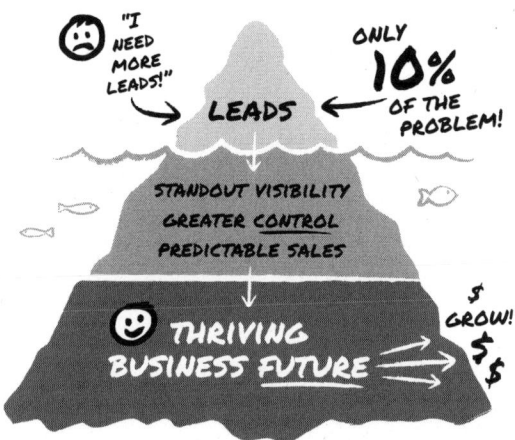

This is what you need to be focused on achieving, and this is why I created a framework – a practical, logical, how-to that takes you through the process of becoming the market leader and reaching a new level of power at the bottom of the iceberg. It's all in the RED Method.

Imagine having a business that attracts clients effortlessly, gives you complete confidence in your lead flow and delivers predictable, profitable results with every sale.

What would this look like for you? Picture yourself running a business where you're not constantly chasing leads. Instead, clients are coming to you, drawn by your standout reputation. You wake up each day knowing exactly where your business stands and where it's headed. There's no anxiety about where the next customer is coming from – you've got a clear view of your pipeline.

And the best part? You've got your numbers dialled in. You know to the penny what each lead costs, what it takes to convert them and exactly what profit you'll make. It's not just about having more customers – it's about having a predictable, profitable system that works for you.

How would that change your day-to-day? The stress that melts away, the confidence you'd feel in client meetings, the freedom to focus on growth and innovation rather than constantly worrying about keeping the lights on. That's the power of building a solid foundation for your business, rather than just chasing leads.

I believe in you. I also believe that you deserve outrageous success and the good news is, with the right mindset – one that embraces technology and automation, focuses on the right things and is committed to continuous improvement – it's within your grasp.

Avoiding the trap of 'hope marketing'

Today, the whole process of selling online can feel extremely challenging. Everything is happening at incredible speed and the digital space is full of conflicting advice of varying quality. For the average business owner, online advertising can feel as imprecise as throwing mud at the wall and seeing what sticks. It is like flying blind, having no idea where you're heading until you get there; like playing darts blindfolded, hoping you'll hit the bullseye.

ADOPTING THE WINNING MINDSET

I also see many businesses 'dabbling' in marketing and advertising – a bit here, a bit there. Or worse, they partake in reactive marketing, where they see their sales pipeline go dry, so they panic.

I call this 'hope marketing', and in reality it is this ridiculous, mostly unconscious marketing strategy that so many small businesses typically employ. If you're a business owner, it is easy to just 'wing it' in marketing, without a plan. You're not measuring anything and you're basically just throwing money at Facebook, Google and any other channel that catches your eye, hoping that something, anything, will work. Sound familiar? If so, you might be guilty of a bit of hope marketing.

The problem with this kind of marketing is that it's a total waste of time and money. If you're not planning your marketing efforts, you're not learning anything from your mistakes. If you want to get real results, you need to ditch the hope, the inconsistency and reactivity, and get strategic.

This means taking the time to understand your target market, crafting messages that speak directly to their needs and desires and mapping out clear, measurable steps for your customer journey. Once you've created a strategy, we can look at your system. Does it effectively capture leads, cultivate them and convert them into sales? With a proven strategy operating through a successful system, you can scale your business by reaching new audiences, retaining customers to resell to them, and continually refining your approach. There are nine accelerators that put power into your automated sales machine: markets, messaging, mapping, capture, cultivation, conversion, reach, reselling and refinement as the book progresses. We'll come back to these as we work through the book.

If you, like so many others, are guilty of hope marketing, don't worry – the good news is that there is very little randomness to digital marketing. Professionals create and stick to a plan. There is always a method to the madness, and I'm sharing mine.

The Revenue Growth Formula

Let's cut through the noise about growing your business. Everyone's always chasing the next shiny new object, distracted by advertising and social media content making big promises and missing what really matters. But the reality is, there are only four ways to boost your revenue. Yes, just four.

When I started out, I was bombarded with advice from all sides. It was overwhelming. But over time, I figured out it all boils down to this:

1. Leads

2. Conversion rate

3. Average sale value

4. Purchase frequency

ADOPTING THE WINNING MINDSET

To have the right mindset, you need to be focused on the right things. These are the four 'dials' of your revenue growth and if you crank up any of these, you'll generate more revenue. Crank them all up and you'll crack the code to serious growth.

So here's the simple formula:

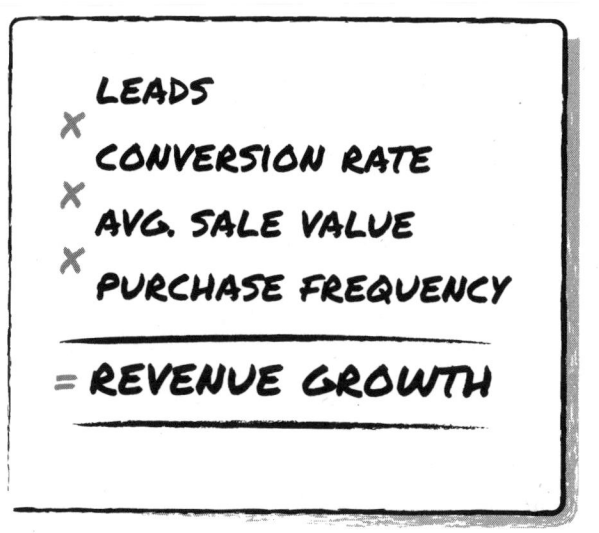

```
    LEADS
  x
    CONVERSION RATE
  x
    AVG. SALE VALUE
  x
    PURCHASE FREQUENCY
  ─────────────────────
  = REVENUE GROWTH
```

No MBA required. It's a straightforward game plan to take your business to the next level. Let's break it down:

- **Increase leads:** More leads mean more potential customers. Simple as that. Everything is downstream from leads. You have to focus on traffic. It's all about putting your business in front of more people, via both paid and organic methods. Paid traffic is like hitting the gas – quick results, but at a cost. Think Google or Facebook Ads. Organic traffic is more like planting seeds – it takes time (which is also a cost), but it pays off long term. Invest in SEO, content, and social media; mix it up to keep your pipeline full.

- **Increase conversion rate:** Leads are great, but worthless if they don't buy. Your conversion rate is the percentage that do. Make it stupidly easy for people to buy from you. Streamline your website, train your team, follow up fast. Use a good CRM to stay on top of things. The smoother the process, the more sales you'll close.

- **Increase average sale value:** This is the average amount each customer spends per purchase. Make each sale count. You've done the hard work in getting them – now maximise it. Upsell and cross-sell – you don't have to be pushy, but if you don't make offers, no one can buy from you. Offer premium versions or complementary add-ons. Show them the value in upgrading or adding on. It's about educating, not hard selling.

- **Increase purchase frequency:** This is how often your customers return. You want to keep them coming back because loyal customers are gold – they spend more over time and bring in new business. Focus on reselling, reactivating dormant customers, and getting referrals. Set up a loyalty programme, stay in touch through email and social media, and give incentives for referrals. Happy customers are your best marketing.

It's simple, but powerful. It takes focus and consistency, but the RED Method will show you ways to crank up all four of these dials to grow your revenue.

2
Future-Proof Your Business

If you're aiming to become a market leader, you will have to change, adapt and innovate the way you think about marketing. This has always been true, but today, change needs to happen more quickly and be more radical than ever. Why? Well, technology, in the form of digitalisation, social media, communication, artificial intelligence and more, is disrupting our lives at an ever-increasing rate. The rules keep changing. We, as mere human beings, simply can't keep up with the rate of technological change. Our brains are the same old brains we've had for hundreds of thousands of years. Now, keeping up, let alone getting ahead, can feel like an immense challenge.

For example, who would have predicted we'd have devices in our pockets combining digital photography with online shopping, booking taxis, paying taxes, ordering takeaway food, running business accounts, hosting online conferencing and more? We are facing continual, radical and bewildering change.

The challenge for you, as an ambitious business owner, is that you can't just sit back and do things the way you've always done while the marketplace is steaming ahead with technological advancements. If you are just observing and not innovating, your business is most likely already on a steady, slow decline. Standing still means being eaten up by competitors who, through new technology, can take more and more market share from you until there's nothing left.

How should you respond to this existential threat? Well, staying static won't protect you in our modern, technology-driven world. You need a change of mindset. Believing that 'it will all work out in the end' isn't a safe, nor an effective growth strategy.

One of the reasons we humans get stuck in our ways is the assumption that our past defines our future. We take comfort in what we know. Habits are hard to break; behaviour is difficult to change. Yet doing more of what you know works here and now isn't going to get you where you want to be tomorrow. Every new level of growth requires a different set of strategies and tools. The strategies and systems you used to reach $500,000 are different to those that you would use to grow your business to $1M, and so forth.

Thriving in our rapidly changing, technologically advanced marketplace means actively applying smart new things in your business that produce effective outcomes. The risk is that otherwise, you get trapped in complacency and are prone to inertia and inaction. This is when newer, faster and more agile technology-driven competitors can quickly encroach on your market share. And why shouldn't they? They're using the right tech, strategies and systems (like those we cover in this book) as their secret sauce. They move faster, they're more visible and they provide better customer experiences, so why wouldn't they overtake you? Imagine (or maybe you don't have to) the frustration of watching your competitors growing steadily, when it could be (and should be) you.

Where are you now?

Do you know where you are in your business growth journey? To grow your business to the level you truly desire, you need to be clear on where you are today and where the gaps are that you need to fill to get ahead.

In looking at your overall business journey, it's useful to set some goals. Remember our three critical outcomes? Let's look at those in more detail:

1. Standout Visibility
2. Greater Control
3. Predictable Sales

Businesses need to be seen. Standing out gives you the best opportunity to work with more customers and clients. Business owners want the calm, clarity and confidence that come from earning steady revenue around the clock; this means control. Predictable sales make it easier to plan for the future and make investments into your business.

I have developed a tool to help businesses identify how they are performing against these three targets. It sets out four zones, or levels, you might be operating in. These vary from leading the way at the top, to being too exhausted to fight the good fight at the bottom.

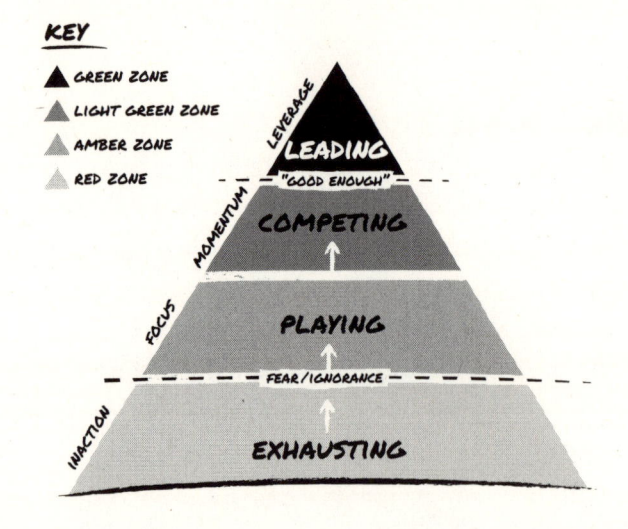

KEY
- ▲ GREEN ZONE
- ▲ LIGHT GREEN ZONE
- ▲ AMBER ZONE
- ▲ RED ZONE

LEVERAGE — LEADING
— "GOOD ENOUGH" —
MOMENTUM — COMPETING
FOCUS — PLAYING
— FEAR/IGNORANCE —
INACTION — EXHAUSTING

Exhausting

Sadly, too many people and businesses are trapped at the lowest level, exhausted. This is a hamster wheel situation, with owners stuck with a lot of 'doing' yet getting very little reward for their efforts. They have no predictable system to bring in new customers, which makes the day-to-day stressful and the future uncertain. Their businesses are typically also invisible online as they are too busy to create content, yet they're getting drowned out by aggressive competitors. They are often beaten by more competitive offers and constantly getting pushed down on price. Let's face it, it's not a good place to be for too long (although most of us have started out there), as it can result in burnout and despair.

The thing is, being stuck at this 'exhausting' level is sometimes not your fault. People can easily find themselves trapped below the fear and ignorance line. Then it's like the system is working against them. What keeps people and businesses down at this level is fear, stress and confusion. This gets them stuck in a vicious cycle of doing a lot of work but going nowhere.

You see, people at this level buy into the myth that referrals and word of mouth are enough, and they fail to innovate or invest in their business because they think it's too expensive, too much like hard work or not worth it in the long run. They lack ambition, and hold a limiting belief that their desired future (more money and freedom) isn't even possible. With this book, I want to challenge that myth and help you recognise the truth: that with the right marketing strategies and systems, you can almost immediately jump up to the next zone.

Playing

At the next level up, we tend to see businesses who are more hopeful, sales trickling in with a moderate but growing brand awareness, but they're still very reactive. I sometimes like to call this the 'following zone', as these people are closely watching what others are doing.

They're still fighting fires, dealing with cash flow, recruitment and service delivery, but they're generally running a tight ship. The good news is, they know they need to invest in marketing and systems; their challenge is finding the time (and the right people) to put it all in place. They are actively looking around for tools, technology and marketing ideas, because they know what they need to do: invest in the growth of their business. When it comes to their brand visibility, they're hopeful that they are becoming well known in the market, and they're considering investments into their website and other advertising methods. Sales are coming in, albeit a little randomly, and they spend most of their time managing the chaos.

They come to realise that to get to the next level they're going to have to make a concerted effort to crack the lead generation code. Daniel Priestley, a well-respected business guru, memorably said, 'Everything is downstream from leads.'[2] This means

---

2   ScoreApp, 'Daniel Priestley on how everything is downstream from lead generation – Expert Empires' (1 November 2022), www.youtube.com/watch?v=ntBYPkqXOtA, accessed October 2024

putting in place the right methods. This focus drives them forward to the next stage.

Competing

In the light green zone, you'll often see that businesses start to see a return on their investment into the right things. Their brand is somewhat known in the market, their lead generation efforts are producing a steady stream of leads and they're using some systems and software to analyse data and gain control.

This stage actually feels pretty good. It's starting to feel like you have a business here and not a job. This zone is where businesses are, at last, competing. But to keep moving up through this level you need momentum.

A funny thing happens when we work with people and businesses at this level. They hit what I call the 'Good Enough Line'. On the Good Enough Line, you buy into the myth that 'We're doing OK and OK is good enough.'

The truth is that 'good enough' traps you. Good enough is not disaster-proof – just look at what happened to many businesses in the Covid-19 pandemic. What if Steve Jobs at Apple had created the iPod and then said, 'Well, that's good enough'? Another company would have created the iPhone and iPad (by different names, presumably), and Apple would not have become arguably the greatest company in the world. Think about it another way. What if you were buying a product or service and the company selling it to you said, 'We're going to try and do a good enough job' – how would you feel about that?

If you become complacent, satisfied with your business just being 'good', it can prevent you from putting in the extra effort required to make it truly great, truly outstanding. And that's what it takes to lead in today's market. One of my great mentors, Tony Robbins, similarly emphasises that being merely 'good' is often insufficient for long-term success and growth.

'Good' won't help your business stand out and differentiate itself from competitors in a crowded market. These days, businesses need to strive to be exceptional and deliver unique value to capture market share. Believing that 'good' is enough can stifle your creativity and innovation, which will stop you from ascending any higher in our pyramid.

Leading

At the top of our pyramid are the market leaders; these guys are continually seeking to improve their offerings, processes and business models to stay ahead of the curve. Great market leaders provide outstanding, memorable and personalised customer experiences that build loyal brand advocates. They are continuously optimising their processes and looking for ways to streamline, increase efficiencies, innovate and improve operations. At this stage, business leaders cultivate a mindset focused on solutions, growth and possibility rather than limitations. This mindset shift pushes them past 'good enough' into the top level of the pyramid, where they can achieve breakthrough results. Being 'good' is a great starting point, but it's not the endpoint.

As you look at the four business levels I've devised in my model and think about where you are right now, imagine what it would be like to move to the top. The RED Method is the trampoline that will take you to the top and make your business the first choice. Step by step, my proven methods will elevate your business into the top 1% of businesses leading your market. They will bring the calm, clarity and confidence you've been looking for when it comes to investing in the levers and accelerators of the RED Method, which will turn your business into a predictable, money-making machine. It will set the tone for the next ten years and beyond.

But before we look towards the future, it's helpful to understand what's gone before and where we are now in the grand scheme of history.

Business in the Fourth Industrial Revolution

I'm not sure whether you got the memo, but we are living through the Fourth Industrial Revolution.

But let's rewind. Every revolution had its own unique way of generating wealth and radically transforming the world. The First Industrial Revolution began in Great Britain in the late eighteenth century. It was the period in history that saw the development of machinery and the birth of automation. Goods were produced in steam-powered factories rather than handmade in homes or on farms, fundamentally changing how economies worked. Before this revolution, labour was almost entirely devoted to agriculture, and wealth came primarily from land ownership, which led to a great divide. If you owned land, you amassed money; if you didn't, you worked the land to provide for yourself and your family. With early industrialisation, innovators began earning wealth for themselves, independent of land ownership.

Next up was the Second Industrial Revolution, which lasted from the 1870s to the outbreak of World War I. During this period, advancements in steel production, electricity, the internal combustion engine, the telegraph and the railways all developed at a rapid pace. Assembly lines began supplying mass-produced products to global markets, enabling innovators to generate more wealth than ever before.

For example, the Ford Motor Company, founded in 1903, was soon producing hundreds of thousands of Model T Ford cars each year. Before the Model T? Well, the horse was the prevailing mode of personal transport. There were around twenty million of them working across the USA in the early 1900s. And people *loved* their horses. In 1912, a New York City banker was said to have commented, 'The horse is here to stay. I am convinced that automobiles are a novelty – a fad.'[3] By the 1920s, however, they were toast. Streets that had once been filled with horses and carriages were now dominated by automobiles. Stables and blacksmiths were replaced by garages and mechanics. All-consuming industrial capitalism had been born.

The Third Industrial Revolution is sometimes known as the Information Age. Some claim it began with the invention of the transistor in 1947. Others suggest the first computing technology of the 1960s. Either way, it was dominated by the rapid expansion of electronic communication and computing. By the 1970s, radio, television and telephones became inexpensive and ubiquitous. Computers existed as large, specialised machines used by businesses, universities and government agencies rather than the public. This seemed to suit everyone for a while. In 1977, Ken Olsen, the founder of Digital Equipment Corporation (DEC), a leading mainframe computer manufacturer, famously said that he could not see a reason for any individual to have a computer in their home.[4]

Yet, just a few years later, in 1982, *Time* magazine named the personal computer its 'Machine of the Year'.[5] This signalled the PC's arrival as a transformative technology, much like the Model T decades

---

3 ST Bushnell, *The Truth About Henry Ford* (The Reilly & Lee Company, 1922)
4 Interview with Gordon Bell by David Ahl, *Creative Computing*, 6/4 (April 1980)
5 'Machine of the year 1982: The computer moves in', *Time Magazine* (5 October 1983), https://time.com/archive/6697864/machine-of-the-year-1982-the-computer-moves-in, accessed October 2024

earlier. It was the personal computer that ushered in the next wave of capitalism.

Work, however, was still very much task-based. We did one thing at a time. We picked up the telephone to speak to someone. We used a computer to compute. We used a hammer to bang in a nail. In many ways, work hadn't evolved at all.

This brings us to the Fourth Industrial Revolution, sometimes abbreviated to IR4 or referred to as 'Industry 4.0.' It marks the point at which, for the first time in our history, there is a blurring between the real and the technological worlds. Like it or not, the digital landscape has become a holistic space in which to do business. We have a generation for whom the term 'digital native' has been coined. Constant connectivity is now so deeply embedded in our lives that it is no longer possible, or useful, to differentiate between online and offline existence. To return to our burger chain example, today we are as likely to order a home-delivery Big Mac from an app on our phones as we are to walk into a restaurant.

In the early days of IR4, which began in the mid-twentieth century, most machines were designed for a single, specific purpose. Telephones were for making calls; hammers were for striking nails, and so on. Each tool had its own distinct function. However, as digital technology advanced, a new type of machine began to emerge: the multi-purpose machine that the PC became. Unlike their single-purpose predecessors, these modern computers could be programmed to perform a wide variety of tasks, from simple calculations to complex simulations.

The growth of Computer Aided Design is an example of this in action. Although aircraft manufacturer Boeing had created a 'computer graphics' department as early as 1962, the multi-purpose hardware to make digital design universal wasn't available for another thirty years. With the growth of cost-effective desktop PCs, the same machine could do your accounts, type your letters and produce design drawings. In industry, the same computers were soon also powering automated production and distribution lines. Digitalisation had truly begun. By having a single machine perform multiple tasks, computers and similar technologies revolutionised business, communication, entertainment and virtually every other aspect of modern life.

The shift from single-purpose to multi-purpose machines represents a fundamental change in how we interact with technology. It's a shift that has defined IR4 and continues to shape our world today.

Throughout history, each era or revolution has been characterised by unique ways of generating wealth. In the agricultural era, wealth was primarily generated through the cultivation of land and the production of crops and livestock. The Industrial Revolution saw the rise of factories and mass production, with wealth being generated through the manufacturing and sale of goods. The Information Age, ushered in by the advent of personal computers and the internet, saw wealth being generated through the creation, processing and dissemination of information and digital services. Now, in IR4, we are seeing a new paradigm of wealth generation.

With the rise of artificial intelligence (AI), the Internet of Things (IoT) and other advanced technologies, wealth is increasingly being generated through the development and deployment of smart, connected and automated systems. These systems are transforming industries, creating new business models and unlocking previously untapped sources of value. As in previous eras, those who are able to harness these new technologies and adapt to the changing landscape are likely to be the winners in terms of wealth generation.

This means that leveraging technology is not optional. Those businesses who don't do it will eventually stagnate and die. It's not enough to have a great product. It's not enough to be good at what you do. If you are serious about thriving in today's economy, you will need to face your fears, implement tech and continually develop your sales system. Jeff Bezos, the founder and CEO of Amazon, described the situation by saying, 'What's [very] dangerous is to not evolve.'[6]

In today's market, the line between online and offline commerce has blurred. Consumers now gravitate towards brands that are omnipresent (everywhere), relatable and offer superior value.

---

6   FastCompany, 'Jeff Bezos – "What's dangerous is not to evolve"' (12 February 2009), www.youtube.com/watch?v=2rEW4KFqHZc, accessed October 2024

They form lasting relationships with businesses that earn their trust, understand their needs and provide effortless purchasing experiences. To stay competitive, it's imperative that companies leverage technology to create an effective digital presence. Those who fail to adapt risk losing market share to more agile competitors who will quickly become the consumer's preferred choice.

The good news is that I'm going to be your guide through this technologically radical, digital landscape. The opportunities are massive. The potential to reach all the clients you desire is there. There are lessons to be learned, best practices to adopt and proven tools and technologies to use. Importantly, you can – and should – apply these things right now.

From technician to business owner

In his book *The E-Myth Revisited,* Michael Gerber talks about a common trap many service business owners fall into. He calls them 'technicians' – people who are great at what they do, whether it's plumbing, graphic design, or cooking.[7]

Let's say you're a fantastic accountant. You love crunching numbers, balancing the books and finding clever ways to minimise your clients' tax liabilities. It's what you're passionate about, and it's why you started your own accounting firm in the first place.

---

7   M Gerber, *The E-Myth Revisited: Why most small businesses don't work and what to do about it* (Harper Business, 2001)

But here's the catch: being an excellent accountant doesn't automatically make you a successful accounting firm owner.

Many business owners get stuck doing what they're good at – in this case, preparing tax returns and financial statements – and forget about the other important parts of running a business. This is a big mistake. The hands-on accounting work is only part of what it takes to run a successful accounting business.

As an accounting firm owner, you also need to manage the firm's finances, market your services, hire and train staff, deal with client relationships and plan for the future. You need to wear many hats: accountant, financial manager, marketer, HR manager and visionary.

The problem? There are only so many hours in a day. It's tempting to spend most of your time doing what you're comfortable with – poring over spreadsheets and tax codes – because that's what you enjoy and know best. But if you only focus on this, your business might struggle to grow or even survive.

To really succeed, you'll need to take a step back from your core service and move from business operator to owner. You must learn to leverage technology, automate processes and confidently invest in digital marketing strategies. It's about finding a balance between delivering excellent service and growing your business strategically.

This might mean implementing a customer relationship management (CRM) system to streamline your sales process, or setting up automated email campaigns to nurture leads. It could involve exploring digital marketing channels like search engine optimisation (SEO) or pay-per-click advertising to generate a steady stream of new prospects. Whatever the marketing strategy, your sales funnel will be there to capture, cultivate and convert leads to sales – all the time.

Delegating tasks to team members or even outsourcing certain functions can free up your time to focus on high-level strategy. Investing in tools for social media management or content marketing can help you maintain a strong online presence without consuming all your time.

It might feel uncomfortable at first to shift your focus from hands-on work to these business growth activities. However, it's the key to building a thriving business that can scale beyond your personal capacity. By embracing marketing automation and digital lead generation, you can create a system that attracts and converts clients even when you're not personally involved in every interaction.

Let's take McDonald's as an example. Their solution to achieve business growth was standardised, automated and replicable systems. You may not want to build a global burger brand, or even a national, multi-location business, but the principle for a single business is the same. The more you can standardise, systematise and modernise, the easier things are to scale. Technical activity alone is not enough to build a successful business, so why not get help with the other bits? If you're also willing to leverage technology to do this – well, it's a good thing you're here.

Sales and marketing automation is a key aspect of my model precisely because this helps you, as an owner, move away from being a technician. It gives you more time, space and autonomy to manage leadership tasks. Instead of getting lost amongst the overwhelming and conflicting priorities, you can enjoy your leadership role knowing that your marketing and sales are in hand. Imagine the peace of mind of knowing that you're successfully acquiring new clients twenty-four seven.

Why your marketing doesn't work

The main reason marketing often falls flat for small businesses is simple: they lack a solid plan. Many small business owners treat marketing like an extra chore, only doing it when they have spare time or cash. They stop and start. They might try a bit of everything – a Facebook ad here, a flyer there – without really thinking it through. It's like throwing spaghetti at the wall and hoping something sticks. But this scattergun approach usually wastes money because it doesn't bring in customers. To make marketing work, small businesses need to figure out who they're trying to reach and what they want to say to them, then stick to a plan that makes sense for their business.

Here are some typical reasons your marketing doesn't work:

- **You don't truly understand your customers:** Sure, you might *think* you know who buys from you. But do you really? Let's say you sell air conditioners. It's not just about finding people who want to buy cool air. It's about understanding why they're buying, what they can afford and what worries them about making a purchase.

- **You don't stand out in the crowd.** Many small businesses struggle to explain why they're special. Why should someone buy from you instead of the shop down the street?

- **You stop and start your marketing:** Marketing is like exercise – you need to do it consistently for it to bear fruit. A scattergun approach will not yield consistent, long-term results.

- **It's random, thoughtless advertising.** Some businesses just throw a Facebook ad up one day and send an email blast the next, without any real plan. This is like trying to build a house without blueprints.

- **You're not keeping score (tracking).** Many businesses don't track how well their marketing is working. They might count sales, but miss other important signs that show if they're on the right track.

LEADS MACHINE

POP QUIZ!

Take a moment to think about how well you know your marketing metrics. Can you answer these questions off the top of your head?

1. Do you know exactly where your leads are coming from?
2. Which digital channel is your most profitable?
3. How many leads do you get every month?
4. What is your average cost per lead?
5. Do you know how much it costs to acquire a new customer?
6. What is your monthly advertising spend?
7. What's your conversion rate for bookings from internet leads?
8. How many sales calls/demos/consultations did you do last month?
9. How many did you close and what's your conversion rate?
10. What is your cost per sale?

If you don't know the answers to these questions, not to worry, 90% of your competitors don't either. If you do, congratulations – you're in a great position to improve your results!

Many business owners don't know what they don't know, so it's key to start the thinking process.

Data is the new gold

In IR4, data is the new 'gold'. By pinpointing your most profitable digital channels, you can focus your efforts where they'll have the biggest impact. It's not just about getting *more* leads, but about getting the *right* ones.

Knowing your monthly lead count gives you a baseline to work from. It's your starting point for setting realistic, achievable goals. But leads are only part of the story. Understanding your cost per lead and customer acquisition cost helps you plan your marketing budget.

Your monthly advertising spend is like a gauge on your business dashboard. By comparing it with your results, you can see if you're getting good value or if it's time to shift gears. And speaking of results, your rate of booked calls/enquiries from internet leads is a key indicator of its effectiveness. If it's not performing well, it might be time for a tune-up.

But your cost for leads only matters when leads turn into sales. That's why tracking your sales activities – enquiries, discovery calls, demos, consultations – is crucial. It helps you focus on quality, not just quantity. Your closing rate shows how often you're sealing the deal. If it's not where you want it to be, it might be time to refine your pitch or invest in some sales training.

Finally, knowing your cost per sale gives you a clear picture of your profit margins. It's the bottom line that ties everything together, crucial for your pricing strategies and overall financial health.

By regularly analysing your data, you're not just running your business – you're steering it with precision. It's like having a roadmap and a compass for your journey to success. You'll know exactly where you stand and where you're heading next. In today's competitive market, this kind of data-driven decision-making isn't just helpful – it's essential for any business looking to grow and thrive. We'll delve into all of these metrics in detail later in the book so that you know exactly what to measure, how to put that data into context and then utilise those insights to drive your business forward.

This is not your general 'how to grow your business book'. We are laser focused on marketing, sales and client acquisition. There's no great mystery, secret or formula to it either. My guess is that if you haven't yet built a reliable, predictable selling system already, its's because of lack of clarity.

The RED Method business levers – Roadmap, Engine and Drive – and the nine key accelerators within them, represent a step-by-step pathway for business owners who are looking for a blueprint for marketing and sales success.

Imagine a thriving business future where your sales processes are running like a Swiss clock. You'll finally have the time and space to truly focus on growing your business, spending time with your family, or anything else you want to do with your newfound freedom. No more wasting money on marketing that doesn't work. And with today's technology, it is within your grasp (and budget). The next three parts of the book will walk you through the RED Method, accelerator by accelerator.

Please don't mistake a clear pathway for a shortcut. This is not going to be an easy ride, but it will for sure be an enlightening one. I'm going to help you build assets for your business that will be working to deliver leads, sales and increased visibility in your market, for the foreseeable future. So it's worth doing some deep work.

Automating client acquisition, for instance, requires deep reflection on your customer relationships. In my career working with thousands of business owners, I've observed that very few businesses really take the time to understand their marketplace. While most know enough to get by – with general messaging and broad targeting – only a select few possess the laser-sharp focus and targeted messaging needed for marketing success.

So I'm going to ask you to take a step back, rethink what you 'know' to be true, validate your assumptions and level up your marketing strategy. I'm so excited to be your guide. Your journey to automated sales and business freedom starts here.

3
The RED Method: The Nine Steps To Unlocking Consistent Predictable Sales

Based on what I've seen working with thousands of service business owners across the globe, the number one growth challenge remains constant: the need for consistent, predictable sales.

As a business owner, you've likely experienced the rollercoaster of feast and famine cycles, where periods of abundance are followed by stretches of scarcity. But what if there was a way to smooth out these fluctuations and create a steady stream of revenue? Enter the RED Method.

The RED Method wasn't born in a boardroom or conjured up by ivory tower theorists. It emerged from the trenches of real-world business challenges, shaped by the successes and failures of countless service providers just like you. This method is the distillation of years of experience, trial and error and relentless optimisation. At its core, the RED Method is designed to address the three fundamental outcomes that every service business craves:

1. Standout Visibility
2. Predictable Sales
3. Greater Control

These outcomes aren't just 'nice-to-haves'; they're the lifeblood of your business. But achieving them isn't a matter of chance or luck, it's about pressing the right levers and accelerators in your business machinery.

THE RED METHOD

ROADMAP
CONFUSION → CLARITY!

GREATER CONTROL

STANDOUT VISIBILITY

THRIVING FUTURE

PREDICTABLE SALES

ENGINE
ANTIQUATED ↓ AUTOMATED

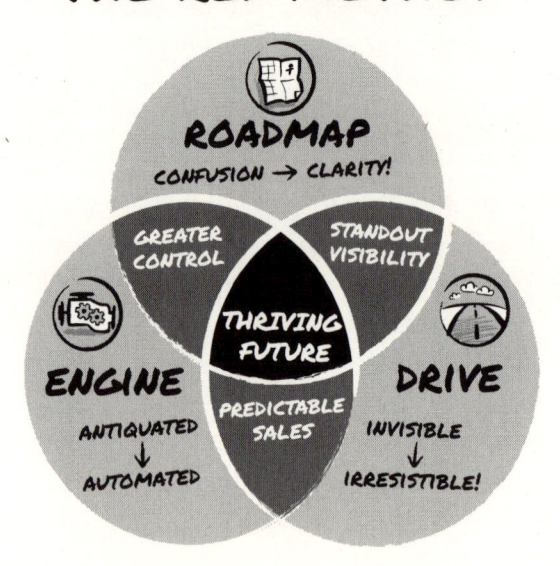

DRIVE
INVISIBLE ↓ IRRESISTIBLE!

Three levers to grow your business

Imagine your business is a high-performance sports car. Like any precision machine, it needs three key things to dominate the track: a clear **Roadmap**, a powerful **Engine** and the **Drive** to win. Let's pop the hood and examine each of these.

Roadmap: From confusion to clarity

Just as no serious driver would race without knowing the track, your business needs a clear course. The Roadmap lever is your GPS and racing line combined, cutting through the fog of daily operations. It transforms your journey from aimlessly wandering backroads – reacting to every twist and turn – to commanding the fastest line through every corner with precision and purpose. This is about moving from confusion to clarity, where every business decision is as deliberate as a perfectly executed racing line.

Engine: From antiquated to automated

These days, manual processes are the equivalent of showing up with a worn-out family sedan at a Formula 1 event. The Engine lever is about transforming your business's power source – replacing clunky, manual gears with a sophisticated, automated transmission. Think swapping out that tired old engine for a state-of-the-art power unit that runs flawlessly twenty-four-seven. While your competitors are still hand-cranking their engines, your business purrs along automatically, converting prospects into customers with the efficiency of a well-oiled machine, even while you're in the pit stop.

Drive: From Invisible to Irresistible

Having the best car in the garage means nothing if you're not in the race. The Drive lever is your ticket to the championship circuit. It's about taking your business from casual track days to the Grand Prix of your industry. This is where we amplify your presence, using digital marketing like a finely tuned exhaust system that makes your brand's voice impossible to ignore. Instead of quietly lapping an empty track, you're commanding attention in every race, on every circuit where your potential customers gather. That's true omnipresence. Each of these levers acts like a performance upgrade. Each one is powerful on its own, but just as a championship car needs the perfect combination of components working in harmony, these levers reach their full potential when enhanced with the right accelerators. Think of them as your high-octane fuel – the elements that turn a fast car into an unbeatable machine.

Overview of the RED Method accelerators

Before we dive into the nuts and bolts of each lever, we need to understand a key concept in the RED Method: accelerators. Think of these as high-octane fuel for your business engine. In the context of the method, an accelerator is a specific tool, strategy or methodology that amplifies the effect of a lever.

Each lever in the RED Method has three associated accelerators, so we have nine in total. These accelerators provide an actionable framework to follow, helping you achieve results faster and more efficiently than you could by using the levers alone. They are designed to answer the questions: 'What goes into a great strategy?', 'What does an efficient system consist of?', 'How do I scale my business and get more people to know I exist?'

The RED Method accelerators are practical, actionable elements that you can implement in your business. They're not theoretical concepts – they are battle-tested strategies and tools that have been proven to drive real results. They have been used by hundreds of our clients to produce millions in sales. They work synergistically with their respective levers to create a powerful system for generating consistent, predictable sales.

By applying these accelerators, you're essentially pressing the fast-forward button on your business growth. Let's explore each of them in detail.

THE RED METHOD

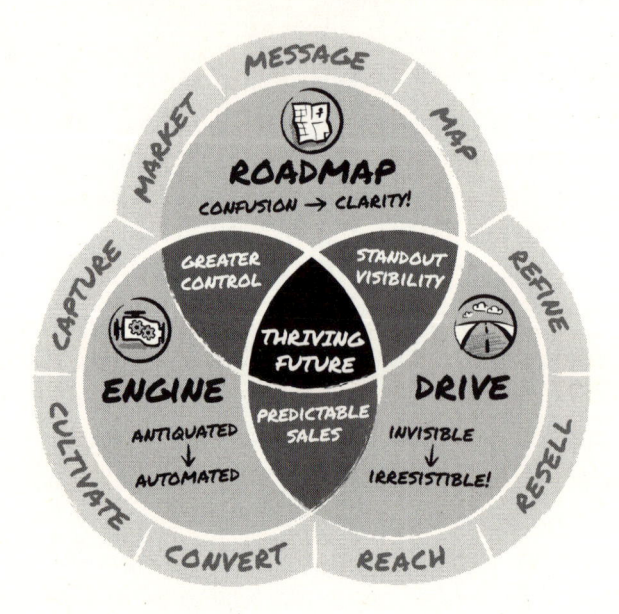

Roadmap accelerators

1. Market: The Smart Market Insight Framework™
Understanding your market is like having a crystal ball that allows you to see into your customers' minds. The Smart Market Insight Framework helps you uncover the hidden desires, fears and motivations that drive your ideal clients. Armed with this knowledge, you can create marketing messages that resonate on a deep, almost instinctual level.

THE RED METHOD

2. Message: The Magnetic Messaging Method™
In a world where customers are drowning in noise, your message needs to cut through like a lighthouse beam in the fog. The Magnetic Messaging Method helps you craft a message so compelling that your ideal clients can't help but be drawn to you. It positions you not just as a service provider, but as the go-to authority in your field.

3. Map: Market Mapping Framework™
The journey from prospect to loyal customer isn't a straight line – it's a winding path with many decision points. The Market Mapping Framework helps you lay out this journey, ensuring you're delivering the right message at the right time, to the right people, guiding your prospects towards making a buying decision.

Engine accelerators

4. Capture: The SmartCapture System™
In today's crowded and diverse digital landscape, leads flow in from a wide range of sources, creating a management and sales challenge. Businesses are missing out on sales and leaving huge amounts of revenue on the table. The SmartCapture System integrates all lead sources into a single, cohesive system, automating tagging, tracking and team notifications. In my experience, this accelerator typically boosts lead capture rates by 30–40%, streamlines operations

57

and provides valuable insights for smarter marketing decisions and personalised customer interactions.

5. Cultivate: NurtureNet™

Most prospects don't buy on first contact, often requiring multiple touchpoints to convert. According to Marketing Donut, 80% of sales require five follow-ups after the initial contact and only 2% of sales are made during the first point of contact.[8] I created The NurtureNet accelerator to automate this process, consistently reaching out with personalised content across various channels. This 'always on' nurturing approach helps prospects get to know, like and trust your brand, significantly increasing engagement and shortening sales cycles while your team focuses on high-value interactions.

6. Convert: ConversionCatalyst™

Turning interested prospects into paying customers is the ultimate goal of your sales process. ConversionCatalyst streamlines this crucial stage, automating follow-ups, providing timely reminders and delivering persuasive content at critical decision points. Leveraging AI-powered sales assistants, this system guides prospects through a frictionless buying journey, increasing conversion rates by

---

[8] R Clay, 'Why you must follow up leads' (Marketing Donut, no date), www.marketingdonut.co.uk/sales/sales-strategy/why-you-must-follow-up-leads, accessed October 2024

10–20%, reducing sales cycle length and ensuring no opportunity slips through the cracks.

Drive accelerators

7. Reach: Reach360™
To grow and scale, more people need to know you exist. The Reach360 accelerator is your blueprint for digital omnipresence, combining paid advertising with organic growth strategies to ensure your brand is visible at every touchpoint in your ideal customer's life cycle.

8. Resell: Remarket Method™
As we covered in the Revenue Growth Formula, one of the best ways to increase your revenue is to increase the frequency of purchase. In fact, it's much easier to sell to existing clients and warm prospects than to strangers. Your existing customers are your most valuable asset. The Remarket Method helps you tap into this goldmine, increasing purchase frequency and reactivating past customers to maximise their lifetime value.

9. Refine: MetricsMaximiser™
You can't improve what you don't measure, so establishing and optimising those KPIs (Key Performance Indicators) is essential to maintain steady, sustainable growth. The MetricsMaximiser is our unique methodology to continuously measure and

improve your marketing and sales machine, ensuring you're always getting the best possible return on your investment.

Putting the RED Method to work

The true power of the RED Method lies not in its individual accelerators, but in their synergistic interaction; each relies on the others to function optimally. To get where you want to go, you need a roadmap, an engine and the drive to keep moving forward.

By following the RED Method you will be implementing a holistic approach to business growth that addresses every aspect of your sales and marketing process. It's about creating a self-reinforcing cycle of growth, where each success catalyses the next, propelling your business forward with ever-increasing momentum.

Your journey begins here

In the chapters that follow, I'll dive deeper into the accelerators, equipping you with practical, actionable steps to implement the RED Method in your own business. Get ready to transform your business from an unpredictable sales roller coaster to a consistent and predictable Leads Machine.

Just a word of caution: I've already explained that the RED Method is not a 'magic pill' that will revolutionise your business overnight. Instead, it's a framework for establishing the right systems and processes to build a rock-solid foundation for sustainable growth. Think of it as a roadmap for a thousand-mile journey. Each step you take guided by the RED Method is another mile down the right road.

PART TWO
YOUR MARKETING ROADMAP: FROM CONFUSION TO CLARITY

A well-crafted marketing strategy is the cornerstone of any automated system driving consistent, predictable sales. Over the next three chapters, we'll develop your roadmap using the first three critical accelerators:

1. **Market** – Master Your Market To Become The Go-To Authority

2. **Message** – Craft Irresistible Messaging That Converts Customers Into Action

3. **Map** – Design A Journey That Builds Trust And Drives Sales

As a business owner, you're bombarded with competing priorities and overwhelming decisions. The key to cutting through this noise is gaining clarity. By mastering these three accelerators, you'll be forming an overarching strategy for your marketing and sales machine giving you a clear path forward.

A clear understanding of these three aspects of your business is the bedrock of so much that follows. Together, they will provide a well-defined marketing strategy based on a clear understanding of your market and target audience. A good marketing strategy begins by defining your ideal clients, their needs, preferences, behaviours, pain points and more. It looks carefully at your competitors too. Where can you gain a competitive advantage? Where are the opportunities to differentiate your brand and your offers?

Off the back of identifying and describing your target audience and analysing your competitors, you can carefully craft meaningful marketing messages and compelling offers that will help your business stand out, resonate with your audience, gain attention and, ultimately, get clients to buy from you. Taking the time to work on your strategic roadmap ensures your messaging is consistent across all channels and your brand conveys the trust, recognition and authority you need it to.

I love helping my clients nail their marketing strategy, avoid costly mistakes and succeed, as the below case study shows.

CASE STUDY: Help Me Fix – the automated recruitment funnel that took them from startup to scale-up

When Ettan Bazil founded Help Me Fix, he had a revolutionary vision: to create the 'Uber for home repairs'. They're bringing remote diagnosis to homeowners, connecting them with skilled contractors to diagnose and fix minor issues in their home. But like many innovative startups, Help Me Fix faced a critical challenge that threatened to derail its growth: how to consistently attract qualified engineers to their network.

By implementing the RED Method, Help Me Fix underwent a significant business transformation that caught the attention of industry veterans and peers alike. The results demonstrated the power of a properly considered roadmap in solving critical business challenges.

We didn't just create a recruitment strategy; we revolutionised Help Me Fix's entire Roadmap so that it pointed towards growth. Here's how:

- Recruitment reimagined: We flipped the script on traditional hiring, treating recruitment as a cutting-edge marketing campaign.
- Laser-focused targeting: We developed a detailed engineer avatar so precise you could almost reach out and shake their hand.
- Magnetic messaging: We crafted compelling copy that spoke directly to engineers' hearts and minds, making Help Me Fix impossible to ignore.
- Funnel mastery: We built a step-by-step recruitment funnel so effective, it practically pulled qualified engineers into the network.

The impact on Help Me Fix was transformative:

- Lead generation on steroids: The funnel consistently delivers leads at an astounding £2.83 each, making engineer recruitment consistent and predictable.
- Scalability: They wanted to grow faster, so we turned up the dial. Help Me Fix can now control its growth with near-surgical precision.
- Time liberation: Ettan went from constant recruitment worries to having so much free time, he had to find new issues to solve (a nice problem to have).
- Built to last: Three years on, and this recruitment powerhouse is still going strong without Ettan breaking a sweat.

- Knowledge explosion: The team didn't just get a funnel; they got a masterclass in marketing strategy that continues to pay dividends across the business.

What made this funnel a runaway success? We knew where we were going from the start, because we had a great roadmap. By investing time in truly understanding the ideal engineer and crafting a message that hit home, we created a system that worked from day one and still works efficiently even years later.

The RED Method is built for transformation. By creating a sustainable asset that continues to deliver results years after its implementation, Help Me Fix bypassed the usable startup challenges and catapulted themselves into a new league of business growth.

With their recruitment pipeline now a well-oiled machine, Help Me Fix has been free to focus on innovation and expansion. They're not just growing – they're redefining what's possible in the home repair industry.

In committing to a well-structured and well-thought-through marketing strategy, you are planning and putting in place a long-term vision, or map, for your marketing efforts. It will help you to anticipate future trends, challenges, opportunities, and threats and adapt your approach accordingly. An overall marketing Roadmap also forces you to measure results and track the performance of your marketing initiatives. Is it taking you to where you want to go? It's a vital question to keep asking. Data-driven decisions around optimising your efforts will lead to better results both in the short and long term.

4

Accelerator 1: Market – Master Your Market To Become The Go-To Authority

The first accelerator of your Roadmap lever is all about getting to know your market. To create standout marketing that cuts through the noise, you need to gain an in-depth understanding of who your market is and how they behave. We do this with the Smart Market Insight Framework, a powerful tool I have developed that will help you identify and analyse three core components of your market:

1. Ideal customer avatar

2. Competitor landscape

3. Market awareness and sophistication

Do you really understand your market? I mean truly, deeply, intimately? This exercise is for everyone, whether you've been in business for decades or are a startup just getting off the ground. The market changes, customer buying behaviour changes and the competitive landscape changes, so it's always valuable to take some time and recalibrate what you think you know about your market.

How effectively does your marketing capture and address the core desires and pain points of your target audience compared to your competitors?

1	2	3	4	5	6	7	8	9	10
Barely Noticed			**Somewhat Relevant**				**Targeted Excellence**		
'Our marketing efforts fail to make an impact or address customer needs.'			'Intermittent success in marketing points to considerable untapped potential.'				'Our marketing precisely targets market needs, standing out sharply from competitors.'		

If you do this work, you're already ahead of 99% of your competition. What you learn and create through this accelerator you will use in your marketing, sales messages and communication strategy for years to come.

Popular men's skincare brand the Dollar Shave Club is widely celebrated as an example of business that deeply understands their audience. Launching a new razor brand into an already saturated market dominated by massive brands such as Gillette and Wilkinson Sword immediately positioned Dollar Shave Club as a plucky underdog. Their launch campaign centred on a low budget but hilarious online video that featured their CEO mocking the shaving industry's established practices. It offered an alternative, a new way to purchase blades via a technology-enabled online subscription model. As their launch video went viral, it became clear that they had decided to use humour to stand out and this resonated with a younger audience. They dramatically disrupted their market, attracted millions of subscribers and forced the big brands to re-evaluate their own pricing and sales strategies.

The success of Dollar Shave Club underscores the significance of having a well-defined roadmap and marketing strategy. The company's journey began with gaining a deep understanding of their target audience through comprehensive market research. This enabled them to craft a message that resonated strongly with young consumers seeking a convenient and affordable shaving solution. Starting with audience research is essential for developing relevant messaging in a roadmap.

Despite entering a saturated market, Dollar Shave Club differentiated itself through a unique subscription model and a humorous approach. This clear and distinct value proposition allowed the brand to disrupt the industry, highlighting the importance of focusing on a unique selling point in a strong marketing strategy.

Consistency in messaging played a crucial role in Dollar Shave Club's success. The brand's launch video went viral due to its concise and relatable content. A well-planned marketing strategy ensures that the brand's identity is reinforced through consistent messaging, effectively engaging the target audience.

In summary, a roadmap that incorporates thorough audience research, a clear unique value proposition and a consistent messaging strategy is vital for creating impactful marketing campaigns, especially in competitive markets. Dollar Shave Club's experience serves as a valuable case study, emphasising the importance of these key elements in building a thriving brand. We can all learn from timeless examples like Dollar Shave Club. Service businesses are typically operating in highly competitive markets, and finding ways to cut through the noise, be different and get people to notice you is a challenge. On the other hand, I could find many examples of marketing strategies that didn't work because the company didn't understand their market. One of the most recent comes from a global multinational corporation who you'd think would know better.

In 2017, Pepsi ran an ad campaign that was widely considered an epic fail. It featured celebrity influencer Kendall Jenner attending a protest march and apparently saving the day by offering a can of Pepsi to a thirsty policeman. The ad was criticised for trivialising social justice movements such as Black Lives Matter and Extinction Rebellion. By appearing insensitive to the genuine struggles of protestors, the campaign completely missed the mark on understanding the cultural context and the seriousness of the real issues troubling their target market. Their hunch seemed to be that young people would be swayed by celebrity culture alone. Nobody, it seems, did the market research to check their strategy. As a result, widespread criticism and a wholly negative social media response meant Pepsi pulled the ad and apologised. Estimates put the wasted production and media buying budgets into the hundreds of millions of dollars. Pepsi's stock price took a tumble in the aftermath too.

It just goes to show how easy it is to lose your marketing money, so taking the time to understand your market and the messaging that will resonate with them might cost a bit more in the short term, but will save you thousands (if not millions) in the long term.

I'm asking you to do genuine research to avoid exactly the kind of situation that Pepsi found themselves in. Time spent here will avoid huge amounts of pain, angst and importantly, a *lot* of money wasted on marketing that doesn't work. By helping you understand these elements, my framework helps you cut through the noise, connect with your target audience and achieve lasting success in today's competitive marketplaces.

Defining your ideal customer

When you *really* know your target audience, you can craft marketing messages that resonate with them. This helps your brand connect with them on a deeper level and stand out from competitors.

We need to understand not only who they are, but also how they make decisions. We need to dive deep. We want to uncover their specific pain points, fears, desires, needs and daily frustrations. What keeps them up at night? What are they secretly longing for? What obstacles do they face? Where are they experiencing difficulties?

We use a specific set of questions, inspired by Dan Kennedy, one of my mentors and the world's leading direct response marketing expert, to help you really get inside your audience's head to understand what drives them. They go beyond surface-level demographics and explore the psychological and emotional aspects of the customer's life. Each question serves a specific purpose in uncovering key insights:

- *What keeps them awake at night, staring at the ceiling feeling anxious and ruminating?* This question will help you discover your market's most pressing concerns, worries, and anxieties.

- *Who are they angry at?* This question helps identify the sources of frustration or resentment in the customer's life, which can inform the tone and messaging of your marketing communications.

- *What are their top three daily frustrations?* Understanding the daily challenges and annoyances faced by your target audience can help position your products or services as solutions to their problems.

- *What trends tend to occur in their lives?* Identifying common patterns or trends in your ideal customer's life can provide valuable context for marketing communications and brand positioning.

- *What do they secretly, ardently desire the most?* This question seeks to uncover your target audience's deepest desires and aspirations, which can be powerful motivators in their decision-making process.

- *Do they analyse purchases or choose by instinct?* Understanding your customer's decision-making style (rational vs emotional) can inform the way you talk to them in your marketing and sales.

- *Do they have their own language or jargon?* Identifying specific terminology, slang or jargon used by your target audience will help you create marketing content that feels authentic and relatable.

- *Have they experienced your competition?* Knowing whether your target audience has interacted with competing products or services can provide insights into their expectations and preferences.

Next up, I'd like you to imagine specific scenarios and situations where your customers might be considering buying from you. Here are nine key questions to consider that will help you gain a fundamental background on why your customers buy – or what's stopping them.

- Where are your customers when they buy your product or service?
- How would you describe their situation at the time?
- Are aspects of their current condition causing them distress or frustration?
- How might a future situation be an improvement over their present one?
- What's blocking them from achieving their desired situation on their own?
- How do they express the distress and frustration caused by these obstacles?
- What misconceptions are they holding onto?
- Do your customers have interests that are not commonly shared by others?
- What are the hot topics of interest known only to your customers?
- What insights do your customers have and share?

Your ideal customer avatar

There are lots of ways of capturing customer information (your answers to the questions above), but by far one of the most practical is the development of a customer avatar. A customer avatar is a tool that captures your ideal customer's information across various categories.

The categories that should be covered in your ideal customer avatar are:

- **Demographic information:** Age, location, gender, social class, earnings and more
- **Psychographic information:** Values, interests and personality traits
- **Behavioural traits:** Buying motivations and concerns
- **Pain points:** Problems your service or product could fix
- **Goals and aspirations:** Ambitions your service or product helps with
- **Approach to purchasing:** Role and potential objections while buying

Here's an example of an avatar I completed for a client in the home services market.

Customer name: 'Homeowner Harry'
Demographics:

- Age: 45
- Gender: Male
- Income: $70,000 per year

- Occupation: Middle manager at a manufacturing company
- Education: Associate's degree in Business Administration
- Marital status: Married with two children
- Location: Suburban area, owns a single-family home

Psychographics:

- Values: Reliability, quality service, home improvement, family security
- Interests: DIY home projects, weekend gardening, watching home renovation shows
- Personality traits: Practical, budget-conscious, prefers long-term solutions

Behavioural traits:

- Buying motivation: Seeks trustworthy, professional plumbers who provide high-quality workmanship
- Buying concerns: Wary of hidden costs, poor service, and unprofessional behaviour

Pain points:

- Problem 1: Difficulty finding a reliable plumber who is available on short notice for emergencies

- Problem 2: Previous negative experiences with unprofessional or overpriced services

Goals and aspirations:

- Goal 1: To maintain a well-functioning, comfortable home for his family.

- Goal 2: To establish a relationship with a dependable plumbing service that can handle all his needs, from emergencies to routine maintenance.

Approach to purchasing:

- Objections: Concerned about high service fees, unexpected charges and subpar work quality

- Role in purchase process: Decision-maker, influenced by personal recommendations, online reviews and past experiences

It is likely you'll need multiple avatars to cover different segments of your customer base. The more insights you can gain, the better. It is also useful for a business to gain a clear understanding of the social media platforms they should be communicating on and what kind of messaging might capture their ideal customers' attention and encourage them to engage.

Customer avatars can also significantly influence your sales approach. The key is to align your messaging with the values and priorities of your ideal customers. By addressing potential objections and scepticism through marketing materials such as testimonials or case studies, you can build trust and credibility with your target audience.

Creating a detailed customer avatar, like the Homeowner Harry example, allows you to tailor your marketing messages and sales techniques to resonate with your ideal customers on a deeper level. By directly addressing the specific needs and pain points of your target market, you can significantly increase your chances of success, even in a highly competitive landscape. We will explore effective strategies for crafting targeted messaging later in the book.

For now, if you have clearly defined your ideal customers, we can proceed to the next component of the Smart Market Insight Framework: analysing your market as a whole.

Knowing your competitors

Who are your top three competitors? How do you stack up against them?

If you've been in business for a while, you should be able to identify your top competitors relatively easily. Who consistently wins work over you? Who frequently appears at networking events, trying to charm the same clients? Which competitors do you secretly wish would just go away? If you're fortunate enough not to have experienced the bitterness of losing out to others yet, a simple Google search

ACCELERATOR 1: MARKET

can help you identify businesses offering the same services in your area.

Having competitors in your market isn't something to worry about – it's actually a good sign that you're in a thriving and profitable industry. Competitors show that there's a demand for what you're offering and give you the chance to stand out, innovate and grow. By checking out what your competitors are doing well and where they fall short, you can find opportunities in the market and create a unique selling point that really clicks with your audience.

Competition pushes you to keep improving your products or services, stay on top of industry trends and give your customers outstanding value. Comparing your performance with that of your competitors helps you set realistic goals and track your progress. Plus, collaborating and learning from others in the industry can lead to some great shared insights and best practices.

So, don't sweat the competition. Embrace it as a motivator for success. Focus on what makes you unique, and use the presence of competitors to keep getting better and leading the market. Now let's do the work.

For your top three competitors, note down how they position their products or services. Look for the messages in their marketing. Note down common headlines they use on their websites, in social media posts, for blogs and other online content. Explore as much of their sales materials as you can. The list might include sales webpages, brochures, video sales letters (VSLs), webinars, downloads, whitepapers and more.

For bonus points, why not 'mystery shop' them to learn about their sales process and get a glimpse of their inner workings and take a note of where they do well and where they're falling short. You could call them up, message them via their Facebook page or fill out a contact form. See how they service clients. Do they respond immediately? How do they answer the phone? Do they have a web chat widget on their website? Do they have a lot of five-star Google reviews? Check out their client feedback through online testimonials. What do people have to say about them? These are all things you should write down and use as market intel. This will give you some ideas for how you can improve your own services.

In terms of advertising and offers, think about:

- What claims do your competitors frequently make to the marketplace?

- What promises do they give prospective clients?

- Do they have a 'unique mechanism'? (We'll get into this later, but in a nutshell it's a 'branded' feature within a product or service that differentiates them by addressing a particular customer need or problem.)

- Are they running ads? What do they say? How do they present themselves? What offers are they running?

> **PRO TIP**
>
> Did you know that you can literally 'spy' on thousands of your industry competitors' Facebook and Instagram ads to see what they're offering and what ads they're using?
>
> The Facebook Ads Library is a searchable database of all the ads currently running on Facebook and Instagram. It's a tool that anyone can use to see what kind of ads are out there, who is running them and what they're about. Let's say you're curious about the types of ads your competitors are using, or you want to check out ads from a specific brand. You can just hop into the Facebook Ads Library, type in the brand name and boom – you'll see all the ads they're running. It's super helpful for getting inspiration, keeping an eye on the competition, or just staying informed about the latest trends in advertising.
>
> It's totally free to use, and you don't even need a Facebook account to access it. Just go to:
>
> > www.facebook.com/ads/library
>
> It's there for anyone to use, but not many business owners know about it, let alone take advantage of it, so there you go.

Here's another way to find a competitive advantage. When you're researching your competitors, make a note of areas where you can gain an edge over your competition – you don't always have to disrupt or radically change your market, as we'll learn below.

Establishing your 'marginal utility'
Why should people buy from you and not your competitor?

There's a concept in economics called marginal utility. The idea is basically to get just that little extra benefit from something small. In marketing and sales, it's about finding those tiny tweaks or additions that make your product or service more appealing than the competition's.

Here are ten examples of marginal utilities that could give you a competitive edge, without you having to completely redesign your product or service:

1. **Price:** Can you offer different pricing structures, eg annual packages or flexible options?

2. **Quality:** Can you improve the quality or durability of your product?

3. **Speed:** Can you provide quicker delivery or service times?

4. **Features:** Can you include a bonus item or feature, like free accessories or added functionality?

5. **Convenience:** Can you offer easier purchasing options, like one-click buying or subscription services?

6. **Customer service:** Can you provide superior customer support, such as twenty-four-seven availability or personalised assistance?

7. **Packaging:** Can you use eco-friendly or more attractive packaging?

8. **Customisation:** Can you allow customers to personalise their products?

9. **Loyalty programmes:** Can you implement rewards programmes for repeat customers?

10. **User experience:** Can you create a more user-friendly website or app interface?

Sometimes, all you need is to be just a little better, faster or to provide better value in one part of your business. You're looking for a small advantage, a tiny difference that can give you the upper hand. For instance, if you're an accountant, you might beat the competition simply by offering a free initial consultation or a faster turnaround time on tax returns. It's a small difference, but it could be a game-changer.

Once you've found your competitive edge, you're on your way to standing out and making new connections with customers and clients. And they're who we'll focus on next.

Building your market visibility

Chances are, unless you're selling something that's truly never been done before (congratulations, you're a genius!), your target market will have a degree of awareness of the problem you're offering to solve and your potential solutions. They'll also have a certain degree of sophistication when it comes to making buying decisions.

Today's consumers are more informed, discerning and demanding than ever before. In an instant, they have access to a wealth of information at their fingertips and can easily compare options to find the best fit for their needs and preferences. This means that understanding your market demographics and desires alone is not enough. As markets mature and competition intensifies, consumers are less swayed by generic marketing claims and more attuned to the nuances that differentiate brands. Sophistication is about understanding the subtleties of customer needs and crafting marketing strategies that speak to them in a refined and targeted way.

As the market is constantly changing, business owners and marketers must stay on the pulse of evolving customer preferences, market trends and competitive dynamics to develop true market sophistication. This requires a commitment to continuous learning and adaptation. Marketers must evolve and stay agile, adjusting their approaches based on data-driven insights and feedback. Sophisticated marketers view their relationships with customers as an ongoing dialogue rather than a one-time transaction.

In his book, *Breakthrough Advertising*, Eugene M Schwartz describes marketing to mass desires as the 'public spread of a private want'.[9] You see, deep down, most people have similar basic desires and needs. We

---

9   E M Schwartz, *Breakthrough Advertising* (Prentice-Hall, 1966)

ACCELERATOR 1: MARKET

might not always admit it out loud, but we all want things like love, acceptance, success and comfort. The trick for us as business owners and marketers is to tap into those private wants and show how our product or service can fulfil them. It's all about understanding what makes people tick at a human level. If you can do that, you can create marketing messages that resonate with a huge audience. You're basically saying, 'Hey, I know what you secretly want and I've got just the thing to help you get it.'

We're all mere humans after all, and at the basic level, we all have fundamental issues, sometimes known as 'domains of concern', that must be taken care of. Putting basic biological and financial needs aside (we all need shelter and food etc), these needs are often what drive our behaviour.

Tony Robbins, the famous life coach and motivational speaker, talks about six of them:[10]

1. **Certainty:** The need for safety, stability and predictability. People want to feel secure and have some control over their lives.

2. **Uncertainty or variety:** The need for change, excitement, and novelty. People crave stimulation and new experiences to avoid boredom.

3. **Significance:** The need to feel important, needed and worthy of attention. People want to be recognised and feel that their life has meaning.

---

10 T Robbins, 'Discover the 6 human needs' (TonyRobbins.com, no date), www.tonyrobbins.com/blog/do-you-need-to-feel-significant, accessed October 2024

4. **Connection/love:** The need to feel connected to and loved by others. People need to feel a sense of belonging and intimacy in their relationships.

5. **Growth:** The need to develop, expand and improve. People have a desire to learn, grow and become better versions of themselves.

6. **Contribution:** The need to give beyond ourselves and make a difference. People want to feel that they are making a positive impact and contributing to something greater than themselves.

In my experience, the need for certainty and significance are the most prevalent. In business, people want to feel certainty (about money, wealth, more customers, security) and significance (recognised, important, valued), so if we can position our product or service as the conduit of those, we are in a great place.

Every feature of your product or service must satisfy a human need. Think about Fitbit fitness trackers. They're not just about the tech; they cater to our need for certainty by giving us control over our health. Tracking steps, calories and heart rate helps us see our progress, which ties into our need for growth as we set goals and improve. Plus, hitting those fitness milestones makes us feel significant and proud of our achievements.

Amazon Prime is hugely popular because it takes care of multiple human needs. The promise of fast, reliable shipping gives us certainty and predictability

ACCELERATOR 1: MARKET

in our online shopping. The vast selection of products caters to our need for variety, with endless new items to explore. Their refund policy is another great example of meeting customers' needs for certainty and simplicity. If you're not satisfied with a purchase, Amazon makes it easy to return items and get a refund. This hassle-free refund policy gives customers peace of mind, knowing that if something goes wrong, they can quickly and easily get their money back. Remember marginal utilities – Amazon is the master of these, which is how they continually dominate their market.

A cybersecurity consultant is a great example of meeting human needs in a business-to-business context. They provide certainty by securing businesses against cyber threats, making leaders feel safe and in control. They help with growth by keeping up with the latest security trends and teaching clients how to improve, fostering a culture of learning. They boost significance by enhancing a company's reputation, making it stand out as responsible and trustworthy, which builds customer trust and opens up new opportunities. Plus, they contribute to the wider digital world, creating a safer internet for everyone. People don't buy cybersecurity solutions, they buy certainty, growth and significance.

See what I'm getting at?

In 100% of situations, you're not selling your product or service at all. You're taking care of people's fundamental human needs. Your marketing has to reflect that, or it's guaranteed to miss the mark.

By understanding the human needs that drive mass market desires, marketers can more effectively tap into the collective psyche and create products and messaging that resonate. Whether it's the need for certainty, significance, variety, connection, growth, or contribution, successful mass market products often align with one or more of these core human motivations.

Now think of your own example. What's the one thing people in your market want the most, or most urgently? How does your product or service give that to them? How does your product or service address your customers' fundamental human needs? You need to figure this out and then base your strategy on it.

By doing the crucial work of identifying your target market's most pressing need and aligning it with your product or service, you'll be well on your way to crafting a killer marketing message that truly hits home. This message will resonate with your audience on a profound emotional level, cutting through the noise and clutter of today's crowded marketplace.

Market awareness

Recognising what level of awareness your potential customers have about your product, service or the problem it solves, is crucial to creating a marketing strategy that works and communication that drives engagement and conversions.

Most businesses have an 'awareness' problem. The simple truth is that if more people knew you existed,

ACCELERATOR 1: MARKET

you'd have more sales. Take the most famous chain restaurant in the world as an example. It's difficult to argue that McDonald's produces the world's tastiest hamburgers, right? Yet they have 40,000 stores worldwide. Why? It's not the product. They have burgers that are arguably OK but they've made systematising and marketing their product the number one priority. As a customer, you know what you will get every time you walk under their Golden Arches, anywhere in the world.

Does McDonald's ever stop advertising? Of course not. But if they're the world's most recognisable burger chain, why do they keep doing it? Because if they stop or slow down, they will quickly lose their market share. Burger King is right behind them, watching their every move…

Remember, the goal of your automated marketing machine is to guide potential customers through a buying journey, from initial awareness to making a purchase, with minimal manual intervention. That means you need to provide them with the right information at the right time to establish your brand as a trusted solution to their problems.

There are five different levels of awareness you should consider when analysing the market awareness of your customer base:

1. **Fully aware:** Customers have extensive knowledge about specific products, their features, pricing and pros/cons.

2. **Product aware:** Customers know what a product or service does but might not be familiar with detailed features.

3. **Solution aware:** Customers are aware that solutions to their problems exist but may not know about specific product options.

4. **Problem aware:** Customers recognise that they have an issue that needs solving but might not know the reasons behind it or that solutions are available.

5. **Unaware:** Customers don't realise that change or improvement is possible and may be difficult to engage with.

Once you have identified your target market's awareness level, you can tailor your marketing efforts accordingly. For example:

1. In a **fully aware** market, marketing should focus on differentiating the product from competitors and highlighting unique features or benefits.

2. For a **product aware** audience, providing more detailed information about features and demonstrating how the product solves specific problems is essential.

3. In a **solution aware** market, educating customers about the range of available options and convincing them of the effectiveness of these solutions is key.

4. When targeting a **problem aware** audience, you should focus on identifying the root causes of the issue and introducing potential solutions.

5. For an **unaware market**, the primary goal is to raise awareness about the existence of a problem and the possibility of improvement through education and thought-provoking content.

By identifying, understanding and addressing these different levels of awareness, you'll be able to create more personalised and effective marketing strategies that will drive better results.

Speak to your audience where they are

Just like levels of awareness, markets also have different levels of sophistication that evolve over time. Identifying the stage your market is currently in is crucial for developing effective marketing strategies. There are five distinct segments of market sophistication to consider: unsophisticated, new sophisticated, established, complex and saturated markets.

Unsophisticated market

When a new product comes out, people don't know much about it. They might not even know they need it. At this stage, simple marketing that focuses on what the product does works best. Think about the first iPhone – Apple just needed to show people what it could do in order to sell it.

New sophisticated market

As more companies start selling similar products, the market begins to grow. Now companies need to start telling people why their product is unlike others. For example, when Android phones came out, they focused on the ways they were different from iPhones – more customisable and cheaper.

Established market

In a mature, established market, people know the basics about the products on offer. Companies now need to give more details about how their product works and what makes it special. Cars are a good example – everyone knows what a car does, so brands like Volvo focus on specific features like safety to stand out.

Complex market

Some markets get extremely complex, with lots of different features and benefits on offer. In these markets, companies need to provide a lot of information to explain why their product is the best. Cybersecurity software is a good example: it's not enough to just say 'it keeps you safe' – companies need to explain *how* it does this.

ACCELERATOR 1: MARKET

Saturated market

In a saturated, or crowded market, there are so many similar products that it's hard to tell them apart. To succeed here, companies need to come up with something completely new and game-changing. Netflix is a great example – they changed the way we watch films and TV shows when the video rental market was overcrowded.

Do you know the state of your market? How aware are people of the problems that your product or service solve? Can you pinpoint their desires and identify their level of awareness and the market's level of sophistication?

In the next chapter, we are going to take all you've learned about your market and dive deep into crafting an irresistible marketing message. We will identify your USP or 'unique mechanism' and design an offer so good that people will feel like it would be stupid to say no.

> ▶ For exclusive *Leads Machine* tools and resources visit: https://francisrodino.com/tools

5

Accelerator 2: Message – Craft Irresistible Messaging That Converts Customers Into Action

Imagine being in the middle of a railway station and repeatedly yelling, 'Hey! Look at me!' at passersby. Nobody would care, some people might turn around, but overall, your calls for attention would largely go unanswered, drowned out by the hustle and bustle of life and people's 'busyness'.

Imagine, on the other hand, yelling 'Hey, accountants!' Out of the hundreds of people around you, there will most likely be a handful of accountants. They will hear your call-out, raise their hands and make themselves known to you. You know that by calling them out specifically, any accountants nearby are going to at the very least listen to you. This second example shows a rudimentary understanding of messaging and how to get it right.

What group of people do you want to speak to?

Take a look at your current marketing message. This might be a current email campaign, your website copy, your social media posts or content on any other communication channels. Ask yourself:

How well does your current marketing message stand out in a crowded marketplace and position you as the first, most desirable choice?

1	2	3	4	5	6	7	8	9	10
Barely Noticed:			**Limited Impact**			**Market Leader:**		
'Our marketing blends into the background, often overlooked amidst competitors.'			'Our campaigns capture attention momentarily but fail to leave a lasting impression.'			'Our marketing sets industry standards, with high levels of engagement, loyalty and conversion.'		

Consider this example of a generic marketing message for a solar company (most service businesses advertise like this):

Save money with solar panels today!

Now compare it with something like this:

Residential homeowner in Manchester? Slash your energy bills by 50% with a customised solar solution. For a limited time, we're offering a free energy audit exclusively for you.

If you were a homeowner in Manchester, which marketing message would grab your attention? Of

ACCELERATOR 2: MESSAGE

course, it's the second one, which speaks specifically to its target audience.

With my Magnetic Messaging Method, you can craft a compelling reason for customers to engage with and ultimately buy from you. We'll design:

- Your value proposition 'one-liner'
- Your value stack
- Your unique mechanism
- Your irresistible offer

Your marketing message is how you communicate the value of your service to your target market. Ideally it is a clear, concise, compelling statement designed to persuade potential customers to engage with you and, more importantly, entice them to take action.

Here's the thing. Most service businesses have weak, general messages that fail to grab attention and dilute the effectiveness of their marketing. We live in a noisy online space and it's probably not an exaggeration to say the average attention span, these days, is measured in nanoseconds. If you can't instantly grab people with your marketing message, you'll end up burning through your marketing budget with not a lot to show for it. Despite this, most marketing messages are boring, uninspired and fail to make an impact.

Here's an example of a typical marketing message that we see every day online. It represents about 90% of the content that is constantly being published:

> At Tried & Tested IT Solutions, we provide top-quality services for all your needs. We offer a wide range of IT services, including consulting, management and support. Our team is dedicated to delivering the best service at the best prices. If that sounds interesting, contact us today for a no-obligation free quote or visit our website for more information.
> Tried & Tested Solutions – your trusted partner in IT success.

Sound familiar? I bet it does – because it sounds like every marketing message you've ever heard… boring and nondescript. It is destined to perform poorly because phrases like 'top-quality services', 'best services', and 'trusted partner' are ubiquitous and generic. Consulting, management and support do not speak directly to a specific audience. They don't differentiate Tried & Tested from any other provider in their market. There's nothing unique to win readers' attention. They're just too broad, covering too much ground and failing to address unique customer or client wants, needs or pain points. There's no emotive language and the whole thing feels timid, lacking confidence and assertiveness. 'If that sounds interesting, contact us today' is a weak call to action that does absolutely nothing to compel readers to respond with any urgency.

Ask yourself, based on the copy above, would someone choose Tried & Tested IT Solutions over its competitors? Probably not, right? There is no offer, no incentive, nothing that would actually get people to think, 'This is what I'm looking for, I'm going to buy it now.' This ineffective marketing message is not a good use of the business's money.

A weak marketing message leads to a criminal waste of the powerful market insight work we discussed in the preceding chapter. There's little point in doing all that work to deeply understand who your customers are and what they truly desire, love, hate or get frustrated by if you don't then align your messaging to it.

The tools in this chapter build on your market knowledge to create a powerful message that speaks directly to your target market in a way that grabs their attention. They'll help you clearly define your value proposition and articulate the unique benefits of your products, services and craft it all into an offer too good to refuse. The process starts by defining and refining your value proposition into a simple, short and easy-to-digest statement.

Craft the perfect pitch

Many businesses struggle to clearly and concisely explain what they do, making it difficult to sell their products or services. If people aren't clear on the problem your business solves, how it works and what the ultimate outcome is, your ability to sell will suffer.

Here's a little exercise. If I asked you, as a stranger, 'What do you do?', could you explain it clearly?

Common, boring answers might sound a bit like this:

- **Cleaning business:** 'I run a cleaning business, we clean homes and offices.'

- **IT solutions consultant:** 'I give advice to businesses to help them with their IT.'

- **Home service business:** 'I run a home service business; we fix things around the house.'

Often this is hard because business owners are too close to their business and assume too much about their audience's level of interest. And sometimes we speak to the wrong people. We've all been next to the business owner who misjudges the mood at a party and goes on for too long about their niche interest. We recognise the snooze-inducing 'blah, blah, blah' yet often make the same mistake in our marketing.

So what do you say when someone asks you, 'What do you do?' Like most, you'll probably explain how you spend your day, all the tasks you do and what you are responsible for, but you won't necessarily say what the outcome is. Chances are, what you do is probably far more interesting than it sounds. Yet so many people fail to impress because they focus on the wrong things.

In their book *Marketing Made Simple*, Donald Miller and Dr J Peterson introduced the one-liner concept,

ACCELERATOR 2: MESSAGE

a tool that resonates strongly with marketers.[11] The one-liner is a concise and compelling sales pitch that clearly communicates the problem you solve, who you solve it for and the benefits they gain. This message can be used across all your marketing channels, whether on your website, landing page, Facebook ads, or even in face-to-face networking events.

The one-liner framework has three parts: problem, solution and benefit. If you follow this framework, it's easy to craft a powerful one-liner that cuts right to the core and makes you look good and your product or service interesting.

Let's put this into action with an example of an electrical company that instals electric vehicle (EV) charging units in residential homes:

- **Problem:** 'If you own an electric vehicle, it's not always easy to find a place that's convenient, easy and fast to charge your EV, at the time you want.'

- **Solution:** 'At T&T Home Charging, we install EV charging points directly into driveways and residences, ensuring that cars are always ready to go whenever they are needed.'

- **Benefit:** 'EV owners now have reliable, instant charging for their EV comfortably in their own driveway, making getting to work hassle-free and efficient.'

---

[11] D Miller and J Peterson, *Marketing Made Simple: A step-by-step StoryBrand guide for any business* (HarperCollins Leadership, 2021)

You can then reformulate this into a marketing message. It can also be very powerful to start with a question. Here's the full result:

> If you own an EV, how easy is it to find a place that's convenient, easy and fast to charge your car at the time you want? We know it's a challenge.
>
> That's why, at T&T Home Charging, we solve this problem by installing EV charging points directly into driveways and residences. This convenience transforms the electric vehicle ownership experience. Your car is always ready to go whenever it is needed, making getting to work hassle-free and efficient.

Is that more compelling than simply saying, 'We install EV charging points'? If T&T just says that, they're the same as hundreds of other businesses. With the above, they have a super clear value proposition that speaks directly to their target market: homeowners with an electric vehicle can't easily find somewhere to charge it, T&T installs a charging point at their home, they can get in their car and drive whenever they need to.

Let's take another example, an IT consultancy. Here, the one-liner might be as follows.

> Are you a small to medium-sized enterprise struggling with outdated technology and inefficient systems? Does your IT hamper productivity growth and compromise security?

At Trust IT Solutions, we solve this through system upgrades, cloud integration and ongoing support. We provide SMEs with seamless technology integration, improved performance and the freedom to stay competitive without disruption.

In this case, small businesses struggle with outdated technology, Trust IT offers system upgrades and small businesses remain competitive.

A value proposition 'one-liner' is a tool you can use to communicate what your business does and why it matters to your audience. With it written down, you can start to use it across all your marketing materials. You can put it on your website, in sales emails, base your brochures on it and use it to prompt advertising campaigns. It is incredibly powerful and worth spending time crafting to get exactly right.

But your value proposition 'one-liner' does not talk in *detail* about what you offer your customers, so there's still a bit of work to do to create a compelling complete offer package. For that, we turn to the value stack tool.

Building your value stack

A 'value stack' is a method used to showcase all the desirable aspects of a product or service, emphasising its benefits and features (what the customer gets) in a compelling way that conveys high value and desirability. This is important for your messaging because you need to consider and communicate the value of each element so that you can highlight the total benefits of your product or service.

The ingredients of a value stack include the core product and then bonus products. Here's an example of a value stack for a solar panel installation company:

- **Core product:** Solar panel installation
    - Custom-designed solar energy system tailored to your home's energy needs, including high-quality solar panels, inverters and mounting hardware.

- **Bonuses**
    - **Energy efficiency audit:** A complimentary assessment of your home's energy usage to identify opportunities for additional savings through efficiency improvements.
    - **Extended warranty:** An extended warranty on all solar equipment, providing peace of mind and protection against unexpected maintenance costs.
    - **Solar monitoring app:** Access to a mobile app that allows you to track your energy production in real-time, monitor system performance and receive alerts for potential issues.
    - **Financing options:** Flexible financing solutions, including low-interest loans and

lease-to-own programmes, to make solar installation more affordable and accessible.

- **Energy savings guarantee:** A guarantee that your solar energy system will generate a specified amount of energy each year, backed by compensation if performance falls short.

You see all the great services we've bundled in? These are typically all part of the core and bonus packages, but if you don't extract and communicate the value in terms of benefit, it's not easy for the customer to understand what they're getting and, more importantly, to quantify it as offering huge value as opposed to simply selling a solar panel installation.

Here's the thing, people don't know the value of what you're offering unless you tell them. In reality, a home solar installation package value stack is likely to be more complex than the above example. There are guarantees, timed offers that give buyers a sense of urgency and scarcity and customer calls to action to consider too. Whatever the details, it should now be easy to see how a helpful summary of the offer, perhaps in visual or graphical form, is a useful tool to help you nail your messaging.

This is your value proposition articulated in such a compelling way that it removes any hesitation or objections a prospect might have about buying. Or, in the words of Alex Hormozi, you need to 'make an offer so good people feel stupid saying no'.[12]

---

[12] A Hormozi, *$100M Offers: How to make offers so good people feel stupid saying no* (Acquisition.com Publishing, 2021)

Below are some illustrative examples of more complex value stacks and offerings based on genuine clients.

Company: FitLife Personal Training
Product: 12-week personal training programme
Value stack:

1. **Core product:** 12-week personal training programme (regular price – $1,200)

    - Personalised workout plans

    - One-on-one training sessions

    - Nutritional guidance

2. **Bonus offers:**

    - Free initial fitness assessment (value: $150)

    - Access to online workout library (value: $100)

    - Complimentary meal planning guide (value: $50)

3. **Guarantee:**

    - 30-day results guarantee: 'See measurable results in 30 days, or get a free month of training'

4. **Urgency and scarcity:**

    - Limited-time offer: sign up within the next 14 days to receive a 20% discount (saving: $240)

5. **Call to action:**

    - 'Transform your body today and claim your bonuses! Click here to start your journey and save $240!'

6. **Value presentation:**

    - Total value: $1,500

    - Discounted price: $960

    - Savings: $540

Company: LearnPro Academy
Product: Annual membership to online learning platform
Value stack:

1. **Core product:** Annual membership (regular price – $500/year)

    - Access to all courses

    - Certificates of completion

    - Exclusive webinars

2. **Bonus offers:**
   - Free ebook on learning strategies (value: $50)
   - One-on-one coaching session (value: $100)
   - Access to private community forum (value: $75)

3. **Guarantee:**
   - Learn-or-your-money-back guarantee: 'Full refund if you don't see improvement in 30 days'

4. **Urgency and scarcity:**
   - Limited-time offer: 'Sign up within the next 10 days to receive a 25% discount' (saving: $125)

5. **Call to action:**
   - 'Start learning today and claim your bonuses! Click here to join and save $125!'

6. **Value presentation:**
   - Total value: $725
   - Discounted price: $375/year
   - Savings: $350

Company: Vitality Wellness Coaching
Product: 6-month health coaching programme

Value stack:

1. **Core product:** 6-month health coaching programme (regular price: $1,800)
   - Personalised health and wellness plans
   - Bi-weekly coaching sessions
   - Access to wellness resources

2. **Bonus offers:**
   - Free initial health assessment (value: $200)
   - Complimentary yoga classes for 3 months (value: $300)
   - Free nutrition guide (value: $100)

3. **Guarantee:**
   - 90-day progress guarantee: 'See progress in 90 days or get an additional month free'

4. **Urgency and scarcity:**
   - Limited-time offer: 'Sign up within the next 14 days to receive a 10% discount' (saving: $180)

5. **Call to action:**
   - 'Transform your health today and claim your bonuses! Click here to start your journey and save $180!'

6. **Value presentation:**
   - Total value: $2,400
   - Discounted price: $1,620
   - Savings: $780

Once you have your value stack, it's possible to summarise it in an offer paragraph that you can use in your marketing materials. Again, I have included some examples based on my clients below:

> **FitLife Personal Training** is offering an exclusive 12-week Personal Training Programme designed to transform your body and improve your fitness. For a regular price of $1,200, our programme includes personalised workout plans, one-on-one training sessions and nutritional guidance. Additionally, you will receive a free initial fitness assessment ($150 value), access to our online workout library ($100 value) and a complimentary meal planning guide ($50 value). We are confident in our services and offer a 30-day results guarantee – see measurable results in 30 days, or get a free month of training.
>
> Act now and sign up within the next 14 days to receive a 20% discount, saving you $240. Transform your body today and claim your bonuses! Click here to start your journey and save $540! Total value $1,500, now only $960.

ACCELERATOR 2: MESSAGE

LearnPro Academy is offering an exclusive annual membership designed to provide comprehensive learning and development. For a regular price of $500 per year, our membership includes access to all courses, certificates of completion and exclusive webinars. Additionally, you will receive a free ebook on learning strategies ($50 value), a one-on-one coaching session ($100 value) and access to our private community forum ($75 value). We are confident in our services and offer a learn-or-your-money-back guarantee – if you don't see improvement in 30 days, you get a full refund.

Act now and sign up within the next 10 days to receive a 25% discount, saving you $125. Start learning today and claim your bonuses! Click here to join and save $350! Total value $725, now only $375 per year.

Vitality Wellness Coaching is offering an exclusive 6-month health coaching programme designed to help you achieve your health and wellness goals. For a regular price of $1,800, our programme includes personalised health and wellness plans, bi-weekly coaching sessions and access to wellness resources. Additionally, you will receive a free initial health assessment ($200 value), complimentary yoga classes for three months ($300 value), and a free nutrition guide ($100 value). We are confident in our services and offer a 90-day progress guarantee – see progress in 90 days or get an additional month free. Act now and sign up within the next 14 days to receive a 10% discount, saving you $180. Transform your health today and claim your bonuses! Click here to start your journey and save $780! Total value $2,400, now only $1,620.

You should now feel able to create a value stack and write an offer summary for your own business. However, before leaving this chapter, there are two more things to consider.

Why you need a 'unique mechanism'

The unique mechanism describes the 'how' in how you deliver the result for your customer. It is your distinctive method or process by which you deliver your promised results. Remember, your clients are not just coming to you for a service; they are coming for the result of that service. A 'unique mechanism' is a great tool to help you stand out as a different and superior way of achieving the desired result.

A unique mechanism is especially crucial in a saturated market because it will prevent your product being seen as a commodity, sparing you from being compared to competitors and racing to the bottom on price. Instead, turning your method or your 'how' into a unique mechanism genuinely sets you apart.

ACCELERATOR 2: MESSAGE

When customers come to you, inevitably they're going to want to know what makes you different from the myriad of competitors out there. They are going to ask how you do what you do. The answer? It's your unique mechanism. You can enjoy packaging it, giving it a sexy brand name and making it an enticing proposition.

For my growth marketing consultancy, we use the RED Method as our unique mechanism.

A well-named unique mechanism needs to enhance your credibility and build trust with your audience. It can make your product seem legitimate and proven. Ideally, it should have a scientific or technological air to it. Unique mechanisms are great for creating interest and curiosity. They give people a reason to pay attention to your message because you're offering something new and valuable that they probably won't have heard of before. It moves you from selling, to educating. Any prospects will feel like they're learning something of value and not just being pitched.

Your unique mechanism also allows you to craft a story around your service. It explains how you do what you do and makes your marketing message more powerful. Importantly, it supports your claims. This matters particularly if you are addressing mature sophisticated markets who have become cynical and sceptical. They've been sold to, marketed to and advertised to for a long time. They're bombarded with similar claims. A unique mechanism helps overcome scepticism by providing a fresh new approach. It instils hope and belief that your product just might be the solution they were looking for.

Consider fitness and weight loss, which is surely one of the most jaded markets out there.

> Brand: We can help you lose 10 kilos.
>
> Customer: How?
>
> Brand: Using our brand new 3X Fatloss programme.
>
> Customer: Really? Tell me more about 3X Fatloss!

Now consider personal coaching, one of the most highly saturated markets we have.

> Brand: We can help you achieve your career goals.
>
> Customer: How?
>
> Brand: Using our exclusive Quantum Leap Coaching Method.
>
> Customer: Really? Tell me more about the Quantum Leap Coaching Method!

And so it continues…

Here are some real-life examples of unique mechanisms for service businesses. See if you can find inspiration to create one for your own business:

The Ritz-Carlton – 'Gold Standards Service'

- **Service:** Luxury hospitality
- **Unique Mechanism:** Gold Standards Service
- **Explanation:** The Ritz-Carlton's unique mechanism, the Gold Standards Service, involves a highly personalised guest experience, where every employee is trained to anticipate and fulfil the unexpressed wishes and needs of their guests, ensuring an unparalleled level of luxury and service.

Ramit Sethi – 'I Will Teach You to Be Rich 6-Week Program'

- **Service:** Personal finance coaching
- **Unique Mechanism:** 6-Week Program
- **Explanation:** Ramit Sethi's unique mechanism, the 6-Week Program, breaks down personal finance mastery into actionable weekly steps, combining psychological principles with financial strategies to help clients achieve financial freedom.

Wag! – 'Pet Happiness Index'

- **Service:** Dog walking
- **Unique Mechanism:** The Pet Happiness Index
- **Explanation:** Wag! uses the Pet Happiness Index, a proprietary algorithm that tracks and reports

on a dog's wellbeing during walks. The index provides dog owners with real-time insights into their pet's activity levels, mood and health, ensuring peace of mind.

1–800-GOT-JUNK? – 'No Contact Junk Removal'

- **Service:** Junk removal
- **Unique Mechanism**: No Contact Junk Removal
- **Explanation:** 1–800-GOT-JUNK? offers a unique 'no contact' service, where customers can have unwanted items removed without any direct contact with the crew. This process was particularly appealing during the pandemic, offering safety and convenience while maintaining high service standards.

Each of these examples demonstrates how a unique mechanism can differentiate a service business, making it easier for potential clients to understand what sets them apart and why they should choose these businesses over their competition.

How to craft irresistible offer 'hooks'

Once you've considered your offer, you need to present it as something your customers should buy – and right now. A great offer involves deeply understanding your customers' needs and providing

ACCELERATOR 2: MESSAGE

overwhelming value, making it hard for prospects to say no.

This means strategically presenting your offer in a way that maximises its perceived value and compels your target audience to take action. In marketing terms, perceived value is important. It is only what your customers perceive that matters. If they think that they're getting more, they are getting more. It doesn't necessarily need to cost you, the business owner, more to deliver this.

Up to now, building an offer and message might have felt a bit longwinded. You wouldn't simply place your offer's complete value stack in an ad. Sure, it has all the details, but it's unlikely to grab the attention of your customers. It won't get you noticed. For that, every offer needs a hook.

The offer hook is a crucial element of any marketing content. It's designed to immediately grab the attention of your target audience and spark their interest. Even if you don't do it yourself, you will have certainly seen people scrolling and scrolling through social media, endlessly looking for inspiration and ignoring ad after ad after ad after ad. However, every once in a while there is one that finally gets their attention. Why? Probably because of their offer hook.

This could be purely graphical, or a video, or music based. In all cases, success comes from knowing what the offer hook is and the right way to express it. An effective offer hook will always communicate the unique benefit, value proposition and unique mechanism of your offer quickly and succinctly. It should be bold, striking and memorable. It should prompt engagement and questions. It can be outrageous even, as long as it is genuine and honest.

A 'great offer' hook saves time, removes pain or adds undeniable value. Great offer hooks are always outcome-focused, meaning you don't waste time talking about what you do or how you do it. You talk only about results. This might need some imaginative thinking. A homeowner (as opposed to a tradesperson) doesn't, for example, buy a power drill to drill holes in their walls. If you take your thinking a step further, you'll realise that they buy a drill to put their mother's treasured painting on the wall. If I choose to work with an accountancy firm, it's not because I love accountancy. I pay someone to do my accounting for me because I find it a pain and I'd rather do other things.

Here are some examples of offer hooks for service businesses:

- **Dental clinic:** 'Get a brighter smile in just one hour – 50% off your first teeth whitening session!'

- **Spa:** 'Escape stress and revitalise your body – book today and get a free aromatherapy massage!'

- **Tax preparation:** 'Maximise your refund or pay nothing – our experts guarantee the best results!'

- **Home cleaning:** 'Come home to spotless perfection – first clean half price, satisfaction guaranteed!'

- **Fitness coaching:** 'Transform your body with personal training – results in 30 days or your money back!'

- **Digital marketing agency:** 'Double your leads in 90 days or get 50% off your next campaign – guaranteed!'

These hooks highlight the outcomes the customers desire, such as a brighter smile, stress relief, a clean home or business growth, making it easier for them to see the value in the service offered and feel compelled to act immediately.

In this chapter, I've outlined the key messaging tools you will need to create a strong marketing message that will build your automated sales funnel and put you in the top 10% of your market. Seriously – if you do this, you are already ahead of 90% of your competitors that either don't know about, or can't be bothered to do this work.

Most businesses don't put this level of effort into their strategy – and it shows. Most businesses are stuck competing on price, getting pushed lower and lower, instead of communicating clearly to the right audience and helping that audience uncover the value they're offering.

LEADS MACHINE

Defining your proposition, offer, unique mechanism and hook are tasks for you as the business owner. This is work that's often difficult and expensive to outsource. Once you dial into your marketing message, all your marketing will work better, so this is a crucial early step.

> For exclusive *Leads Machine* tools and resources visit: https://francisrodino.com/tools

6

Accelerator 3: Map – Design A Customer Journey That Builds Trust And Drives Sales

The truth is that most sales funnels and marketing campaigns don't work that well. That's because an effective automated sales funnel consists of a combination of links in a chain. If just one thing isn't right in your funnel, the whole thing can break. That's why we need to understand, element by element, how to get the best out of each component we put in place.

You may have heard the saying, 'People buy from people they know, like and trust.' Mapping out your sales funnel in a way that plays into this principle is how you'll create a loyal customer base that not only sticks around but also spreads the word about your awesome brand. And that, my friends, is the secret sauce you need for long-term sales success.

The goal of a sales funnel is to guide people from the point of hearing about you for the first time, to becoming happy customers and loyal fans. In our Roadmap, this is the specific customer journey that helps guide your customers, pique their interest, show them that you are the obvious choice to buy from and keep them coming back for more. When we automate this, it's like having a sales team working for your business twenty-four-seven.

How effectively are you delivering personalised messages that drive prospects through your sales funnel? Are you doing it automatically?

1	2	3	4	5	6	7	8	9	10
Non-existent			**Hit or Miss**				**Automation Mastery**		
'No automation, leading to extra work and missed sales.'			'Often leading to customer frustration and unpredictable sales growth.'				'Our messages hit right on time, driving peak sales conversions.'		

The automation advantage

So many businesses are struggling to find new customers. They advertise, network, go to events, post on social media and 'meet for coffee'. Chasing and following up leads is a constant effort, costly, time consuming and can lead to burnout.

An automated sales funnel is a digital marketing strategy that guides potential customers through the buying process automatically, from initial awareness to the final purchase, with minimal manual

ACCELERATOR 3: MAP

intervention. Best of all, it all happens digitally and is highly scalable, meaning that once you've plugged in your system, you can add fuel to the fire, increase your ad spend, get more leads and service more customers than you've ever dreamed of.

The automation aspect involves using tools like email marketing software, CRM systems and marketing automation platforms to handle repetitive tasks, personalise communication and track customer interactions throughout the funnel.

This strategy makes the client acquisition process more efficient, improves conversion rates (making your advertising less costly) and provides a repeatable experience for potential customers.

By crafting a map of your sales funnel and making the journey through it easy and automated, you can grow your business and keep the sales rolling in. The six key stages of your sales funnel, or customer journey, are:

1. Awareness
2. Interest
3. Consideration
4. Intent
5. Purchase
6. Retention

AWARENESS

INTEREST

CONSIDERATION

INTENT

PURCHASE

RETENTION

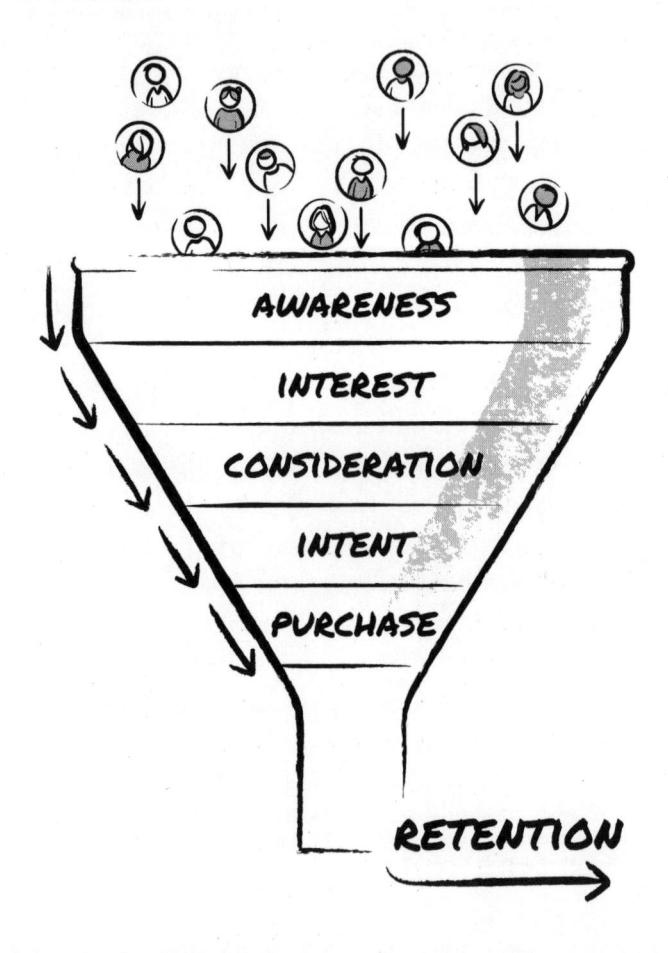

In order to efficiently drive prospects through the stages of your sales funnel, you must master the art of delivering the right message, to the right prospect, at the right time and in the right place, by creating a meticulously crafted customer journey that enhances engagement at each conversion point.

My Funnel Mapping Toolkit helps you understand how you can go from a one-night stand to a lasting marriage with your customers. Before diving in to the details of what each stage entails, however, it's important to understand that not all of your customers are the same, and so it is helpful to segment your target audience.

The 3% Rule: Understanding buyer segments

One of the big marketing mistakes I see businesses make is fighting over the same small group of people who are 'in-market' (ready to buy).

Let's go back to the McDonald's example. Maccy Ds' marketing department will be aware that only a mere fraction of the people who pass their restaurants will buy something. They'll be tracking the footfall (the number of people passing by) for each of their locations.

For instance, let's take their flagship restaurant on Oxford Street, a busy shopping area in London. Hypothetically, McDonald's might estimate that 10,000 people walk past this particular branch in a twenty-four-hour period. However, out of those 10,000 individuals, only around 1,000 (or 10%) might choose to enter the restaurant.

McDonald's likely has data on the purchasing habits of those who do enter the restaurant. They will be able to predict, for example, that out of the 1,000 customers who come in, approximately 250 (or 25%) will opt to buy a Big Mac, one of their signature menu items.

The exact percentage of people who walk by a McDonald's and decide to enter is not widely published information, so we're making wild guesstimates here. But the numbers don't really matter; the point is, even for a highly popular and recognised brand like McDonald's, only a small percentage of the total available market will ultimately become customers. But the company can use this information to make informed decisions about their marketing strategies, store locations and product offerings to optimise their appeal to their target audiences and maximise their sales potential.

These marketing principles apply universally across industries. Whether you're running a global fast-food chain or a local solar panel installation business, the fundamental concept remains the same: only a small percentage of your total addressable market will convert into actual customers at any given time. For instance, even when targeting people actively seeking solar panel installations, you might expect only about 3% to be ready to purchase immediately. Understanding this reality allows businesses to set realistic goals, allocate resources efficiently, and develop strategies to maximise their conversion rates within these constraints.

Of course, it's great to sell to those who are itching to buy from you *right now*, but typically, there's a huge chunk of people out there who just aren't ready yet. You want to build long-term relationships with these folks before they're ready to make a purchase. That's where the real opportunity lies, yet so many businesses ignore it.

ACCELERATOR 3: MAP

The 3% rule identifies five buying categories:

- **3% active buyers:** These folks need a solution now and are actively looking. They plan to buy within the next thirty to ninety days. They're your prime sales leads and should be the focus of your marketing efforts.

- **7% intending to change:** This group knows they need something but hasn't started searching yet. A well-timed campaign or cold call could catch their attention, as they're open to new ideas.

- **30% not enough pain:** These potential customers see the need for your solution but don't feel any urgency to purchase. They might engage with your brand but won't commit until their needs become more pressing.

- **30% no current need:** This bunch doesn't need your product or service right now and isn't responsive to marketing. They might have recently bought something, be too small, or just not be ready yet.

- **30% not interested:** This segment will never choose your brand, no matter what. They might be loyal to competitors, have had a bad experience with you in the past or just prefer other solutions. Focus your efforts on the more receptive segments instead.

LEADS MACHINE

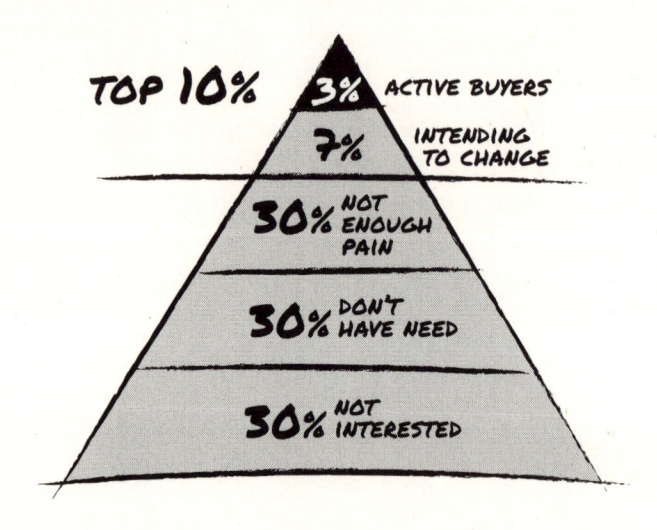

TOP 10%
- **3%** ACTIVE BUYERS
- **7%** INTENDING TO CHANGE
- **30%** NOT ENOUGH PAIN
- **30%** DON'T HAVE NEED
- **30%** NOT INTERESTED

Using the above rule, at any given moment, only 3% of your potential customers are ready to buy. The other 97% either don't know you exist or aren't interested yet – 30% will never buy at all. These are sweeping generalisations of course, but useful figures to have in mind.

Here's the thing: if you can engage and nurture relationships with those that remain *before* they need you, you'll be the first brand they think of when they're ready to purchase. By considering the 67% of customers out there who *might* buy from you, your sales funnel will build relationships with prospects and develop a list of lucrative opportunities that can be nurtured into thousands of future sales.

Just looking for love

A great customer journey is a bit like dating. Imagine the scene: you go out, you're looking for love. You meet a special someone in a bar, and there's that little spark of interest. Ah, *l'amour*! You strike up a conversation, buy them a drink and after five minutes ask them, 'Will you marry me?'

Erm... Kind of creepy, right?

Most likely, they might reply, 'Cheque, please!' and run away, never to be heard from again. It's a sure-fire way to get blocked.

The reality is, if you haven't taken the time to build a relationship, to get to know each other, to create a meaningful connection, asking someone to marry you on the first date is just crazy, right? But that's exactly what businesses do when they shove ads in your face, constantly yelling, 'Buy my stuff! Buy it now!' Like your date, the prospect will be blindsided. They're thinking, 'Seriously, why would I buy from you? I don't even know you, and I definitely don't need you in my life right now.'

On the other hand, if you took the time to wine and dine your prospects, to really get to know them, maybe go on a few 'dates', then, slowly, steadily, over time, you could build that special relationship. And when the moment's right, you pop the question, 'Will you...?' And this time, guess what? They might actually say yes.

This relationship building is what you do with the sales funnel map. It is all about mapping a compelling and effective customer journey that enables you to create meaningful relationships with your potential customers over time (and in the long term). At the right time, when they're ready to buy, you'll already be there.

In the next sections, we'll go through the six stages of the sales funnel, and what you should do for a customer at each stage of their journey to deliver the right messages at the right time.

Note: There's no preconceived timeline for any of these stages; they can take five minutes or five months. It all depends on where someone is in their life or business development, and when that changes.

The six stages of the sales funnel

Awareness

At the awareness stage, people don't yet know you exist. The goal here is to attract a broad audience and make them aware of your product or service (or brand). This is all about reaching as many people as possible and casting a wide net. At this point, you might not even be 'selling' as such, certainly not anything specific. Instead, you could be talking about something relevant to your target market to catch their attention and get them to notice you.

Your ads, content, messages, images – everything you put 'out there' – should address your customers' wants, needs, fears and so on, just as we talked about earlier. There are lots of different kinds of content you can create for the awareness stage.

For a home service business, like a plumbing company, you could share some handy tips on keeping your plumbing in top shape. You could create social media posts about how to prevent your pipes from freezing in winter or how to fix a minor leak yourself. A step-by-step guide on what to do during a plumbing emergency could really grab people's attention too. These would link back to your website or landing page, where you would then capture their details.

If you're a personal trainer, you could create a series of short, fun workout videos for all fitness levels, from beginners to advanced. You could also put together a downloadable meal prep guide to help clients plan their diets and stay on track with their fitness goals.

For an SaaS company offering a project management tool, you could publish blog posts or videos showcasing best practices for managing projects effectively. An eBook or webinar on how to boost team productivity using your software would be a great way to attract and engage potential customers.

Examples of good types of content to raise awareness include:

- Blog articles
- 'How to' guides
- Podcasts
- Social media posts
- Posts in online communities (eg Facebook and LinkedIn)
- Explainer videos

- Infographics
- eBooks
- White papers

Paid ads, social media and SEO all play a part in the awareness stage. As I've already mentioned , the goal here is not to sell your stuff, but to help more people get to know that you exist.

Interest

In this stage, potential customers are 'problem aware' and they're actively seeking more information about products or services that meet their needs. They might not be quite ready to buy yet, but their curiosity is piqued and they're eager to learn more about what you might offer them and if you could be the solution they're looking for. This is your perfect opportunity to engage them further, provide valuable insights and get them hooked on your brand.

This is the stage where the prospect starts to take action and engage with your content. They might follow you on social media, download your lead magnet or subscribe to your newsletter. They could visit your website multiple times, click on links in your emails, or reply to comments on your forum. Taking action is a key part of the interest stage.

Another big part of showing interest is seeking information. Nowadays, customers are used to having all the info they need right at their fingertips – or in their pocket. They could be anywhere and looking up details about you, your product or service and how you can solve their problems.

In the interest stage, customers are checking you out and possibly comparing you with your competition. This could involve making 'micro' commitments, like downloading a resource, attending a webinar, or buying a low-ticket product such as a $9.99 training course or webinar ticket. They're testing the waters, so it's crucial to provide valuable content that educates and informs them. You need a way to bring these interested customers into your world, nurture them, give them the information they want, add value and build trust.

This is a great time to establish credibility through testimonials and customer feedback. Later, in the chapter about reaching audiences, we'll dive deeper into how to build relationships through newsletters, email sequences, drip campaigns, social media campaigns, webinars, live demos and more. But your task at the interest stage of the sales funnel is to provide in-depth information about what you offer and show interested customers how you solve their problem. You will need to think about how you can help customers in this stage learn about and engage with you enough to move to the next stage.

Consideration

The next stage in your sales funnel, the consideration phase, is when prospects who have shown some interest start to evaluate their options more thoroughly. Imagine you're thinking about buying a car. You might start following Tesla on social media and sign up to receive their newsletters because you think Teslas are cool and you like what the brand stands for. You're not necessarily going to buy a car right now, but you're curious. And who knows? Maybe one day…

Fast forward six months, a year, or even two years. Tesla hasn't forgotten about you, and you haven't forgotten about Tesla. You've seen their content, attended a webinar, learned more about electric vehicles, battery charging and what's involved in buying one of their cars. Now, you're seriously thinking, 'I need a new car. Maybe it's time to upgrade.' You start actively researching, comparing different solutions, weighing the pros and cons and seeking out the information you need to make an informed decision.

In the consideration phase, prospects are not just aware of your product; they are seriously contemplating whether you're the best option among all the alternatives. An effective sales funnel will help your business be there (considered) when they're ready to buy. Your brand will be top of mind. The question is, will they buy from you, and are you going to help them to do it? The best companies excel at this – they make buying from them easy.

During this stage, prospects will be searching online. They'll be checking out online reviews, testimonials and case studies. They'll want to see social proof that you're as good as you claim. They'll check out comparison sites, look on YouTube, read or watch virtually anything they can find. They're doing their homework.

Take, for instance, a person thinking about switching to a new smartphone. They might follow tech review channels on YouTube, subscribe to newsletters from Apple or Samsung and read articles about the latest models. Over time, they learn about the features, benefits and potential drawbacks of each option. They might even participate in forums or ask questions on social media to gather more insights.

That's the digital reality we live in. Customers have all the information they need, in their pocket. With new AI tools, they may even have access to intelligent systems to do all the online research for them.

Customers will evaluate your products or services based on features, benefits, pricing and overall value. They'll be looking for unique selling points. The work we did in the last chapter to establish your offer and unique mechanism is crucial here. If customers can't see any unique selling points, they'll think you're just like everyone else. At this stage, they're looking for differentiators that set your product or service apart. And that's the challenge we all face if we're looking to grow and scale online.

They also want assurance that you're reliable and effective. Today, they can find that by looking at online reviews and social proof. If you're a local business, they'll likely check your Google My Business profile first. If you don't have a solid track record of four- and five-star reviews, you're at a disadvantage. Google's algorithms prioritise well-reviewed businesses, so reviews are critical for any business selling online.

The goal of the consideration stage is to educate potential customers and give them the information they need. Show them that your product or service is the right choice, and that it's different – superior – to your competitors'.

Here are some tips to plan out your content for the consideration stage:

- **Share success stories and customer feedback:** Highlight testimonials and case studies from satisfied customers to build trust and credibility.

- **Create comparison charts or guides:** Develop clear, easy-to-understand comparison charts that show how your products stack up against competitors'.

- **Host informative events:** Offer webinars or live demos where potential customers can see your product in action and ask questions in real-time.

- **Provide in-depth content:** Create detailed articles, engaging videos and comprehensive 'how-to' guides that showcase the features and benefits of your product.

- **Implement retargeting campaigns:** Use targeted ads to remind potential customers about your product and keep your brand top of mind as they make their decision.

Remember that this stage is all about building trust and providing value. Your potential customers are actively exploring their options; it's your job to help them make an informed buying decision and, ideally, give them the confidence to buy your stuff.

Intent

When customers reach the 'intent' stage of the sales funnel, they're just a step away from buying from you. They've moved through awareness, interest and consideration, and now they're seriously thinking about making a purchase. They might just need a little more info or a final nudge to help them decide. This is where your irresistible offer comes in. It helps customers take the plunge – whether that's saying yes to a proposal, buying an expensive car, investing in marketing services or hiring a personal trainer. Whatever it is you're selling.

Remember, pulling the trigger can be scary for people, especially for a small business dealing with restricted cash flow, where every buying decision feels like a major step, especially if your product or service is a high-ticket item. At this point, customers are highly engaged with your brand and are looking for final details that will influence their decision – a quote, an offer, a return policy or warranty info. If you're an e-commerce or online platform, they might be clicking around the site and putting things in their shopping cart. They might email you with a query or want to speak to someone directly.

The goal in the intent stage is to convert their interest into action. Make it easy for them to say yes. Sometimes, a final incentive like a last-minute deal, a two-for-one discount, a money-back guarantee or an unexpected bonus at the right moment, can make the difference.

Retargeting ads are fantastic for people in the intent stage. These ads target users who have already visited your website and shown interest. They might already be in your CRM database or receiving your email marketing. We'll cover both of these in the next part of the book.

A retargeting campaign lets you say to your customers, 'We saw that you checked out our website and were wondering if you were still interested in X, Y, and Z?' For example:

> Are you still interested in an electric vehicle charging point installation? We saw that you filled out the form and clicked on some of our content over the last month. To get you started, here's a 10% off code.

Abandoned cart emails work great in the intent stage too. If someone starts the buying process but doesn't finish it, why not send them a personalised offer? Use the data in your CRM to offer incentives or discounts based on the customer's behaviour.

Other examples include:

- 'We noticed you were looking at our premium membership. Sign up today and get 20% off your first month.'
- 'Do you need help finalising your purchase? Live chat with us now for assistance.'
- 'Thinking of purchasing? Read our latest reviews to see why our customers love our solar panels.'
- 'There are only five tickets left for our event! Book them now and we'll upgrade you to VIP status.'

Purchase

The purchase stage is where people put their money where their mouth is and convert into actual clients or customers. This means completing a transaction and buying the product or service. This stage, however, is not only about the act of purchasing. Here you have a unique opportunity to differentiate yourself and provide an exceptional buying experience that will encourage repeat business and customer loyalty.

For example, if you're a yoga studio, you could take the opportunity to create a user-friendly membership sign-up process with secure payment options that make the whole experience seamless. Imagine guiding new members through the process with a welcome message such as:

Welcome to our yoga community! Your membership is now active. View our class schedule and start booking your sessions.

If you're a roofing company, you could create a smooth post-purchase experience for your customers. Once a prospect has made a purchase, you can greet them with something like:

Thank you for choosing ABC Roofing! Your appointment is confirmed. Our team will arrive on [date] at [time]. In the meantime, you can review our project timeline and what to expect during the installation. If you have any questions, please don't hesitate to contact us at [contact information]. We look forward to providing you with top-quality roofing services!

Other examples include:

- 'Your order has been received and your onboarding call is confirmed for the 10th of August, 3.00pm. Our consultant, Katie, will call you.'
- 'Welcome to our community… We can't wait to meet you at the first class. We'll send a list of everything you need to know a week in advance.'
- 'Thank you for ordering our ingredients box and recipe. We have confidence your dinner party

ACCELERATOR 3: MAP

> will be a huge success, so do let us know. Send us photos!'

At our sales automation company, Lead Hero AI, new clients receive a series of welcome emails that tell them how to log in to our tools, give them access to training content and invite them to a one-on-one onboarding call with a marketing expert. This way, we make sure that our customers are set up for success. As you'd expect from us, these are all automated. This saves a massive amount of time and human labour costs.

All of this adds up to a user-friendly intuitive checkout process where the goal is to minimise friction and make the buying process as straightforward as possible. You might have multiple payment options but there should be clear instructions and secure payment gateways to ensure customer security. These are all vital parts of the purchase process.

Think about a restaurant. The ordering and payment process for dine-in customers is streamlined. We all know how paying tableside using a portable card reader works, why not ask for an email too at this point and automatically send a thank you message and collect feedback? For example:

> Thank you for dining with us. We hope you enjoyed your meal. Please take a moment to fill out our feedback form for a chance to win one of our regular prizes.

Home service providers, like plumbers, are also now increasingly providing mobile card readers for technicians to accept payments on site after completing a service, for similar reasons. Business owners can send follow-up emails or texts to confirm the service details and gather feedback:

> Thanks for choosing our plumbing service today. Your payment has been processed. We value your feedback; please take a moment to rate our service.

You can also use this to ensure customers know how to reach out to discuss any follow-up issues:

> If you experience any issues with the work completed, please contact us at [phone number] or [email]. We're here to help.

In a B2B context, the purchasing process can be a bit more complex. You might start with a detailed proposal that outlines the client's needs, or a step-by-step order form to fill out. This can lead into an onboarding process where you gather important info from your clients or ask them to upload necessary materials before scheduling a kickoff meeting.

For the client, they'll go through a sales call to discuss their needs, review a proposal, ask all their questions and then sign a contract online. Many of these steps can be automated to make things smoother. These are all key activities that happen during the purchase stage of your sales funnel. The purchase stage is all about helping your prospects take action, and making sure they have a smooth and positive buying experience.

But the sales funnel doesn't end there. Once you have a client, I'm pretty sure you'll want to retain them for as long as possible. For the purpose of this book, then, the final stage of the sales funnel is retention.

Retention

The retention stage is all about keeping your customers happy, engaged and loyal long after the initial purchase. This phase is crucial for building lasting relationships, encouraging repeat business and turning one-time buyers into lifelong customers. It ensures you don't miss out on the opportunity to delight and keep your clients for the long term.

To return to our romance metaphor, remember you're looking for a marriage, not a one-night-stand. That involves commitment, ongoing communication, providing value beyond the initial purchase and ensuring customers continue to see the benefits of your product and service. This is incredibly important to the success of your business.

The goal of the retention stage in your sales funnel is to keep customers engaged and ensure they always remember you. If they forget about you, they won't buy from you again and you'll have to start all over. This is called 'churn', and it's not fun, resulting in a never-ending hunt for new clients. If you provide a service, you'll know what I'm talking about.

Churn rates across service industries

As a service business owner, you've probably lost sleep over customers who suddenly stop using your services. Especially if you sell a subscription service (like SaaS), or perhaps you're a plumbing and heating business upselling boiler customers onto a monthly care plan, or maybe you're an accountant charging monthly. One day you've got regular, loyal customers (and monthly recurring revenue) and the next, they're gone. This phenomenon, known as customer churn, is a reality for every business.

What is a 'churn rate'? Simply put, your churn rate is the percentage of customers who stop using your service over a given period. It's like a leaky bucket – water keeps flowing out and you need to keep refilling it to maintain the level. In business terms, a high churn rate means you're constantly needing to attract new customers just to maintain your current size, let alone grow. And high churn rates will negatively impact your revenue and lower your repeat purchase frequency (see the Revenue Growth Formula).

Why do customers/clients leave?

First, I must say that churn is a normal phenomenon. It's just a sad reality that clients can leave you, no matter how great your product/service may be and no matter how much you've bent over backwards to serve them. You can't control what they do. There are millions of reasons why clients might leave you that often have nothing to do with you. All we can strive to do is reduce the churn rate by focusing on the things that *do* relate to us, but it will never be zero.

So why do customers leave? One of the biggest reasons is poor customer service. Bad experiences can drive customers away fast. That's why having a well-trained, efficient customer service operation is crucial.

Lack of engagement is also a big one. Customers want to feel connected to your brand, so keeping them engaged with regular updates through newsletters and social media is always smart.

Pricing issues is another one. If customers think they're not getting their money's worth, they'll leave. The market can change, new competitors come along offering what you do better or cheaper (remember marginal utilities), or both. I wouldn't necessarily suggest that you lower your prices, but it is essential to be competitive. Perhaps take a look at your service or see if you can pack even more into your value stack.

How to retain customers

As you can see, dealing with churn is not fun, so keeping hold of customers is vital. One of the components of business growth is increasing the frequency of purchase. This depends on you having customers you can sell to again and again. We will talk more about this when we discuss scaling your business in Part Three.

Even after a purchase, your automated sales funnel keeps on rolling. It shifts gears to focus on keeping customers happy and encouraging them to come back for more. This is where email newsletters come in handy. You can also send thank-you notes, ask for feedback and share extra tips and exclusive offers to boost customer satisfaction and loyalty. Automated workflows can help you upsell or cross-sell products based on what customers have bought before. We'll talk more about this in the next section. Overall, if your communication remains personalised and relevant, you'll gain more repeat business.

Loyalty programmes are another fantastic way to keep customers coming back for more. Just like those famous coffee chains, loyalty points, programmes and discount schemes make customers feel good about spending money with you. People love being rewarded for their loyalty. Invitations to special events, opportunities to give feedback, early access to new features and engaging content like webinars, tutorials, white papers, reports, industry insights and how-to guides all add value over time.

The retention stage of the sales funnel is a continuous process; it's something that becomes part of your business DNA and goes on indefinitely. The good news is, in the next chapters, I'll show you how to automate it all.

ACCELERATOR 3: MAP

Before we move on, take a moment to think about how well your current sales funnel is working. Are any stages missing? Is your brand well known, but you're not converting sales? Or do you have a fantastic product that nobody knows about?

Think about the content you can provide for each stage. Do you have reviews and testimonials? Maybe an eBook? What about videos, blogs, thought-leadership articles or social media posts? This is your opportunity to be creative.

The next part of the book, Engine, is where we'll put together all the elements you worked on in the Roadmap section and start building your automated marketing processes. I hope you're as excited as I am. I love this stuff, because I have seen hundreds of clients' lives and businesses change forever. When the whole machine works, it's magic.

> ▶ For exclusive *Leads Machine* tools and resources visit: https://francisrodino.com/tools

PART THREE
THE ENGINE: FROM ANTIQUATED TO AUTOMATED

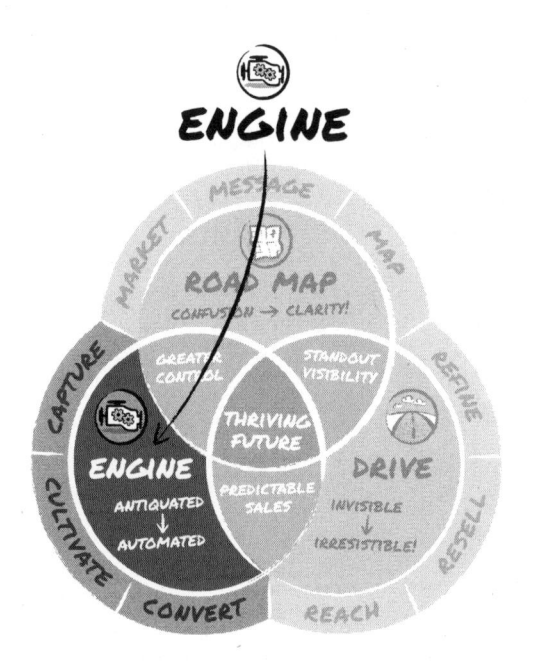

Once you've created your Roadmap, the next thing to think about is the engine that brings that overall strategy to life. The engine is the system that ensures your marketing messages reach the right people, at the right time and in the right place.

The Engine lever is where strategy meets action. I will show you the tools and tech we use to automate your entire marketing and sales funnel. We'll talk about capturing leads, 'cultivating' (nurturing) them and converting them into revenue-generating sales.

In building your Engine, we're going to use three key accelerators that will push things forward:

1. **Capture – Hook Your Ideal Clients With Irresistible Bait.** This is all about attracting leads and capturing contact information from your target audience. We'll cover CRM, landing pages, lead magnets and digital assets that will be working for you to consistently generate a steady stream of qualified prospects.

2. **Cultivate – Nurture Relationships For Lifelong Wins.** This accelerator is focused on cultivating (nurturing) long-term relationships with leads. Once you've won them, we will discuss how you can use content, chatbots, AI and conversational marketing to build that 'know, like and trust' factor. We'll also leverage email marketing, follow-up workflows, segmentation and behavioural triggers to guide prospects towards saying yes.

3. **Convert – Build An Autopilot System To Close Sales.** Here, we focus on how to turn prospects into paying customers. I'll share how to integrate your irresistible offers into your marketing workflows with strong calls to action. We'll learn how to use AI chatbots to qualify and convert leads and book appointments straight into your diary. This will mean you can streamline your sales process and handle any objections your prospects might have without manual intervention.

This is all the fun practical stuff that makes the magic happen and, more importantly, will help you make a lot of money. It's not just theory anymore; we're putting it all into action. In this section, we'll build the machine that will automate, accelerate and grow your business, ensuring it's making sales twenty-four-seven, even while you sleep.

When it comes to setting up automated marketing, the 'engine' is basically the toolkit you use to keep everything running smoothly. It's the combination of tools, steps and software that automatically guides your prospects through their buying journey. The idea is to make turning leads into customers as easy and efficient as possible, without needing to rely on extra manpower – something that our client, The Glow Group, quickly saw the benefit of…

CASE STUDY: The Glow Group – a model of modern business success

There are some great businesses out there that are taking their marketing and sales to the next level through digital automation. One of our amazing clients, The Glow Group – a leading plumbing and heating business in the UK – is a perfect example. They don't just offer quality services; they've also nailed their online approach.

We implemented AI chatbots in their business to convert leads and improve customer experience. Our CRM system helps them to qualify customers efficiently, making sure they're delivering the right service to the right people. Over the last year, they've doubled their team of engineers and seen steady growth.

When you interact with Glow Group – say, asking for a quote or booking a service – you enter a smooth digital system. They're great at following up, whether through email, text or other channels, keeping customers engaged and coming back. Their messages are always relevant and timely, offering value at each step.

What's more, Glow Group has cleverly integrated upselling into their digital strategy.

They use our automated systems to offer care plans to customers, providing an additional service that enhances customer loyalty. For existing care plan customers, they've implemented AI-powered customer care. This means these valued clients get quick, efficient support without Glow Group needing to significantly expand their human customer service team.

This comprehensive approach not only attracts new customers but also keeps existing ones loyal, encouraging repeat business and additional service adoption. And they're not relying on a huge team of marketers to do all this manually. Instead, we've installed an automated system for them that works hard in the background, driving their success.

Let's face it – a lot of businesses struggle with the idea of automated marketing. Especially within the B2B world, many business owners tend to get stuck in their own ways and believe the myth that it won't work for them. 'We're too sophisticated,' they might say. 'Our sales cycle is longer; we sell through relationships.'

If you're in consulting or professional services, you might think your sales funnel has to revolve around in-person meetings, lunches and quick coffees. And for sure, those are great. But how many lunches can you have in a day? Time and geography become real roadblocks.

Today, we operate in a global digital market, with more accessible and cost-effective technology than ever before. This makes it possible to reach thousands, if not millions, of potential customers with your product or services. Additionally, finding small, specific, highly targeted interest groups is easier than ever.

Now imagine having an automated system that lets you have 'virtual coffees' with hundreds of people. No caffeine rush necessary. This will help you to:

- Find better clients without the legwork
- Make smarter decisions based on data
- Work twenty-four-seven to put your business in front of the decision makers you want to talk to
- Reach far more people than you could on your own

If you want to grow a business, automation isn't just a 'nice-to-have' – in this digital era, it's simply a must-have. I have gained literally hundreds of clients, worth hundreds of thousands, via automated systems and I can tell you, it works.

Ready to level up? Let's dive into our Engine accelerators and get you rolling with next level marketing automation.

7
Accelerator 4: Capture – Hook Your Ideal Clients With Irresistible Bait

Getting a consistent and predictable stream of new leads is critical for any business, big or small. The reality is that many websites are simply not built to convert leads effectively. Websites tend to be over complicated, have too many pages and talk too much about the business instead of addressing the prospects' pain points. Crucially, they don't offer any value in exchange for collecting the prospects' details.

Many business owners fail to recognise these issues and websites become more of a digital brochure than a lead-generating tool. By not optimising for lead capture, businesses miss out on valuable opportunities to engage with potential customers and nurture them through the sales funnel.

Remember, data is the new gold. If you're not capturing lead data, you have no way to market to potential clients, build meaningful relationships and, importantly, grow your database of future clients or customers – a resource potentially worth millions. Think of lead capture like fishing. You need the right bait (something attractive to offer), a good fishing spot (where to find potential customers) and a way to reel them in (how to get their contact info).

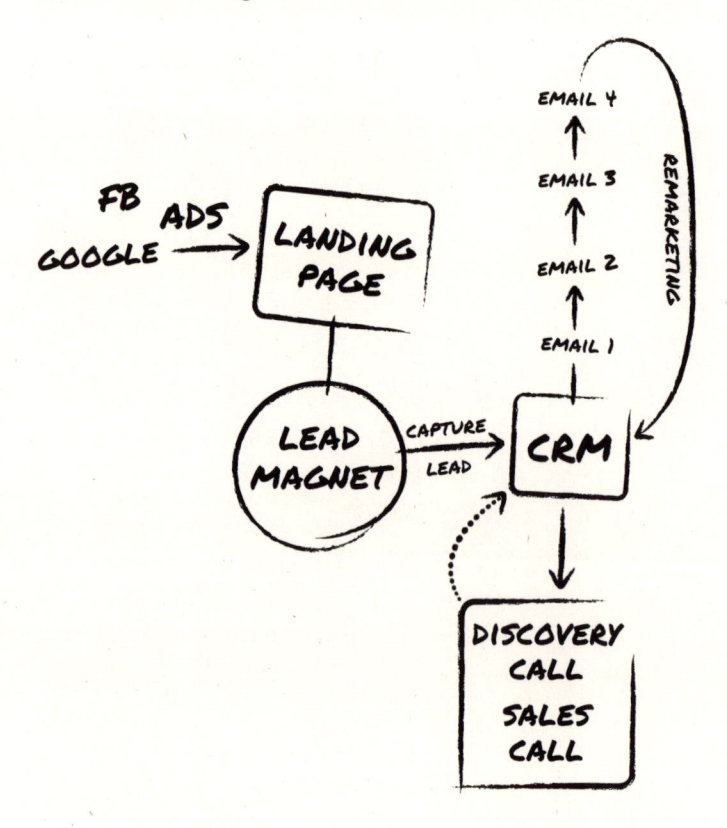

An effective lead capture process is crucial for marketing, sales, and business growth. In this chapter, I'll introduce SmartCapture, a simple system to effectively capture

ACCELERATOR 4: CAPTURE

new leads and use automation to keep this running twenty-four-seven, while you focus on other aspects of your business. We'll cover four main topics:

1. **Lead magnets:** Free 'gifts' to attract potential customers, like an eBook, report, online training or a discount code.

2. **Data and lead scoring:** How to figure out which potential customers are most likely to buy from you.

3. **Landing pages:** These are mini websites with only one purpose – to get the user to take one action (usually completing a form in exchange for a free gift – see above).

4. **CRM (software):** This is your digital 'customer relationship manager' – your little black book for your business, enabling full control over your contacts.

But before we dive in, let me ask you something:

How effectively does your system attract and capture leads, then funnel them into a CRM system for optimised follow-up and sales?

1	2	3	4	5	6	7	8	9	10
No System 'We're struggling to follow up with leads and are missing out on sales.'			**Untapped Potential** 'We have a basic system, but we could be doing a lot more.'				**Lead Magnet Mastery** 'We have a well-oiled lead capture machine.'		

If you're already doing great, the ideas in this chapter will help you optimise things. If your approach leaves a little (or a lot) to be desired, don't worry. I'm here to help every step of the way. It is important to note, there is no way around capturing prospective customer details. As we've already learned, only a small percentage of the market will ever buy from you. We're out to get our little piece of the pie, but first we need to know who they are.

The smart way to capture leads

Capturing potential customer details is important for businesses that want to build relationships, educate their audience and boost sales. So many businesses struggle to make money because they don't collect useful data about their audience and lack (or have neglected to implement) a robust system to stay in touch.

Lead capture is the key first step in creating an automated marketing system that can nurture leads and turn them into loyal customers. By gathering valuable info on who their audience is, what they like, their pain points and behaviours, businesses can create targeted marketing campaigns and personalised offers. This lays the groundwork for a strong, data-driven marketing strategy that can adapt to the changing needs of their target audience and drive long-term growth.

What is a 'lead'?

A lead refers to anyone in your market with the potential to buy from you. To 'capture' a lead you must obtain some basic contact information, such as their name, email address, phone number, or other relevant details, usually in exchange for something of value (a lead magnet), like an eBook, whitepaper, newsletter or free trial.

Leads can be 'hot', 'warm' or 'cold'. Cold leads are people who could buy from you but have had very little or no prior interaction with you. Warm leads are potential customers who perhaps have interacted with your business and engaged with your content enough to know a bit about you. Maybe they've downloaded your free gift, enquired about a service, attended a webinar or commented on a LinkedIn post or similar. A hot lead is someone who has raised their hand and said, 'I'm interested in learning more about you and your product or service.' They've shown intent to buy. They're seeking a solution to a problem. They are 'hot' to trot.

Without a steady stream of leads, you don't really have a business. And without an effective way of capturing and organising your leads, with no way of building relationships and telling people about your stuff, you're making life incredibly difficult for yourself. Having discussed what they are and their importance, next we'll cover tools and tactics for capturing leads. We'll also discuss the use of CRM systems to handle leads once you have them.

Remember, the goal is to automate your lead capture process so that you can enable a consistent, predictable flow of potential customers into the top of your sales funnel.

Lead magnets

The best way to capture leads online is to build an irresistible lead magnet. This is an incentive you offer to potential customers in exchange for their contact information. It's a trade. It's typically free or low cost to you, but it ought to be a highly valuable resource to your customers. It needs to provide a compelling reason for your leads to opt into a relationship with you and freely provide their contact details. It is a permission-based tool to hook people into your business's ecosystem.

Depending on your business, lead magnets might include free lifestyle advice, discounted professional training courses, personal finance quizzes, downloadable industry guides, pre-publication eBooks and more. There are plenty of tools and techniques to choose from. Here are some examples of strong lead magnets:

- **Online self-assessments:** Digital interactive tools that allow users to evaluate themselves on specific criteria often make great lead magnets, especially if you promise personalised results by email. 'How fit are you?' 'Can you afford a house?' 'Are you in the right career?'

- **Checklists:** Simple, actionable checklists that help users accomplish a task can attract leads who have a problem related to your product. A 'New employee onboarding checklist', 'Event planning checklist' or 'Home energy efficiency checklist' are some good examples.

- **Quizzes:** Engaging quizzes that provide personalised results or recommendations can encourage leads to hand over their contact details. For example, 'What's your financial independence score?' or 'Take the Business Resilience Test to mitigate business failure risks'.

- **Training:** Free training sessions, 'how to' videos, or webinars that offer valuable insights or skills can attract high-quality leads. For example, a 'Step-by-step guide to creating effective Facebook ad campaigns', 'How to build an engaging email newsletter in 10 easy steps' or 'Beginner's guide to boosting your website's traffic'.

- **Reports:** Potential customers are often happy to exchange contact details for in-depth reports or industry analysis. Something like: '2024 e-commerce growth trends', 'AI benchmarks and best practices', or 'Emerging technologies in UK marketing'.

- **Whitepapers:** Detailed whitepapers that explore a specific topic or issue in-depth and offer expert knowledge also attract leads. For example, 'The future of digital marketing: Trends and predictions for 2025', 'Maximising ROI with data-driven marketing strategies', or 'Harnessing the power of AI in customer engagement'.

- **Waiting lists:** Why not offer potential leads a spot on a waiting list for new products or services? This creates a sense of exclusivity and anticipation that leads might well be tempted to sign up for. Something like a 'VIP pre-sale', 'Member preview' or 'Sneak preview'.

- **Online community:** Another good way to capture lead details is by offering access to a private online community where users can connect, share insights and receive support.

THE POWER OF QUIZZES AND SCORECARDS IN LEAD GENERATION

Quizzes and scorecards have revolutionised the way businesses attract and engage leads. Unlike traditional lead magnets, they offer an interactive, data-driven experience, delivering instant value through personalised reports or assessments. This approach shifts lead generation from passive to highly engaging, helping businesses connect more meaningfully with their ideal prospects. With the right applications in place, attracting and converting leads has never been easier.

A key tool we regularly use with our clients is ScoreApp, and the feedback has been exceptional. It elevates the traditional lead magnet to an entirely new level. We have found ScoreApp to be a successful tool to:

ACCELERATOR 4: CAPTURE

- **Engage leads** by offering personalised insights, giving them a compelling reason to opt in
- **Create dynamic reports** tailored for each lead, enhancing engagement and building immediate trust
- **Validate new ideas** by building waiting lists and testing interest before launching products or services
- **Capture invaluable data and insights** into what your target market thinks and wants, helping you create more personalised and effective marketing

ScoreApp also integrates seamlessly with HighLevel CRM, creating a powerful system to automate follow-ups, track leads and manage your sales pipeline in one place. ScoreApp has transformed lead generation for several of our clients, helping them capture high-quality leads while delivering genuine value. It doesn't just collect data – it's a tool for starting meaningful conversations and building trust.

To explore ScoreApp, HighLevel CRM and other tools we use to implement the RED Method, visit **francisrodino.com/tools**.

The crucial thing to note about lead magnets is that they should be genuinely valuable to your potential customers. Whatever it is, it should offer real benefits that address a specific pain point or need within your target audience. It doesn't have to be directly related to your flagship or core product; anything that helps make your customer's life easier is worth considering. Your lead magnet shouldn't, however, be any old thing that you put together without thought. Clients will see through a poorly executed, lazy attempt to gain their details. A lead magnet is a chance to demonstrate that you understand your market deeply, and you genuinely want to help in a way that's directly relevant. This should be at the forefront of your mind after completing the Roadmap part of this book.

Data and lead scoring

Once you've created a lead magnet, you need to decide on what information you'll ask for in exchange. An email address is, of course, invaluable but it isn't much use on its own. The more you know about your leads the more you can help them. We live in a data-driven world and collecting information will help you understand your customers, optimise your marketing strategies and, ultimately, increase your sales. The insights you'll gain will allow you to personalise your content and make informed decisions based on your customers' behaviour, preferences and demographics. So don't be afraid to ask a few questions, such as:

- *What's your role?* This will tell you their position and decision-making power.

- *What industry are you in?* Different industries have different needs; this info helps you speak their language.

- *How big is your company?* A solo entrepreneur has different needs to a 500-person company.

- *What's your biggest business challenge right now?* This is gold! It tells you exactly how you might be able to help.

- *Have you used a service like ours before?* This gives you an idea of their experience level and expectations.

- *What's your budget for this kind of service?* This helps you determine if they're a good fit for your offerings.

- *What are you hoping to achieve in the next year?* Understanding their goals helps you position your service as the solution.

- *How do you prefer to learn about new services?* This tells you the best way to communicate with them moving forward.

The more you know, the easier you'll find it to create highly targeted marketing campaigns that resonate with individual prospects. If you know your leads' location or gender, for example, or what they've purchased in the past, you're more likely to be able to advertise to them through the right channels. This will ultimately save you time and money.

Lead scoring is a way of prioritising leads that is more sophisticated than the cold, warm and hot segmentation we discussed earlier. Scoring leads against their likelihood to convert means you can focus on the most promising opportunities first. Giving a particular score or 'tag' to leads who have clicked on a certain page on your website, replied to your emails or ordered similar products means you can control which messages they receive. It's an extremely powerful tool and is a typical standard feature of CRM systems such as HighLevel, for example: www.gohighlevel.com

Landing pages

Where should you promote your lead magnet? A lot of businesses, when they run marketing campaigns, make the mistake of driving traffic to their website. Websites are not typically built to convert leads. They often act more as a showcase for your business, providing a lot of different options and pages. They are a branding tool, essentially, and even a great website that looks flashy and impressive isn't necessarily going to convert leads for you. If you simply send a lead to your website, you can lose the opportunity to capture their details, as two things might be happening: the wrong people reach your website, or the right people reach your website, but they're not finding the lead magnet you promised them and are leaving frustrated. We can get round this problem with a landing page.

This is a standalone web page dedicated to your lead magnet. As part of the sales funnel that we are building, it has one job: to encourage your potential customers to part with their contact information.

To do this, a strong landing page needs five crucial features:

ACCELERATOR 4: CAPTURE

1. A clear main headline that immediately sells your lead magnet

2. Concise copy that focuses on the benefits of your offer

3. A video explainer that speaks directly to the prospect

4. A call to action that shares exactly what you want the visitor to do next – 'download now', 'get your free guide', 'win instant access', 'watch our video'.

5. A simple form with minimal fields to capture data seamlessly.

Here's an example:

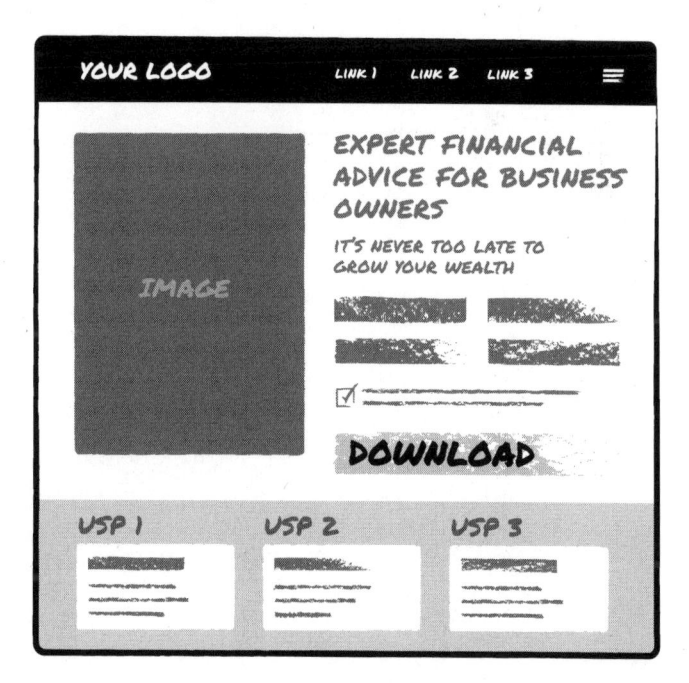

I'm only able to skim the surface of how to create a great landing page in this book, but its purpose is to make your lead capture easy and frictionless. You can always ask your leads for more information later, but in the first instance, less is more so keep the content and questions to a minimum. Having multiple buttons, lots of content and elements can lead to distraction and confuse your prospect. So keep it simple, and remember, if an image speaks a thousand words, then a video tells a million stories.

Often, you can create landing pages through your CRM system.

Your CRM: Stay organised, stay connected, stay automated

A CRM system is like a super-powered contact list for your business. It keeps track of all your customer info and interactions in one place. It allows you to communicate with your contacts and build your database. For service businesses, it's a must-have to stay organised and boost sales.

There are so many CRM software providers on the market, it can be hard to know what to choose. You want something that is easy to use, works with your other tools and fits your budget. Look for one that can grow with your business and works on your phone. Good support is a bonus – because tech can be tricky sometimes.

Integrating your CRM with other software is especially crucial for service businesses. You might

ACCELERATOR 4: CAPTURE

be using dedicated job/field management software, or accounting software like Xero or Quickbooks. Integration capability will save you time, reduce errors and give you a complete picture of your operations. When your CRM talks to your other tools, you're not having to constantly switch between apps or double-entering data.

In our business, and for our Lead Hero AI clients, we use HighLevel as our CRM system of choice. It's perfect for service businesses and has a ton of features and capabilities at a fraction of the cost of other CRMs (many of which may lure you in with 'free' plans that don't do much for your business but get you stuck into expensive long-term contracts based on number of contacts, team members or features).

It is not only great value, but it also provides an all-in-one solution that makes it easy to do everything I discuss in this chapter (and beyond). It can build your landing page, track leads, run email marketing campaigns and more, meaning you don't have to use multiple pieces of software and pay multiple licence fees. Other great CRM systems include Salesforce, HubSpot and Keap.

> **PRO TIP**
>
> As a reader of this book, you can access an extended thirty-day trial of HighLevel by visiting https://francisrodino.com/tools. See how this all-in-one marketing platform can transform your business.

If you don't have a CRM solution yet, I would advise you to do in-depth research based on the exact needs of your business before making a purchase. Beware – it is easy to be seduced by 'free forever' offers, but these are rarely good value for money in the long run. As you expand and market to more contacts, add-on costs hidden in the small print can quickly spiral into hundreds of pounds per month.

If you're not an enterprise-level business and don't have the budget for consultants to build out your CRM system for you, buying an out-of-the-box solution from a major supplier will give you everything you need. Most importantly, it will allow you to manage the process of capturing the data from leads attracted by your lead magnet, organising and segmenting your leads based on tagging or scoring systems that you put in place, delivering the output your lead expects and starting the relationship-building process – all automatically of course!

Lead management

Your CRM is more than just a database. It's your central hub for organising, understanding and engaging with your leads and customers. Here's how you can harness its full potential:

Tagging and scoring leads

Think of tags as labels you can attach to each lead. You might tag leads based on:

- Their source (eg, website, referral, trade show)
- Interest level (eg, just browsing, ready to buy)
- Service they're interested in (eg, for a plumber: water heater installation, pipe repair)
- Location or demographic data

Scoring allows you to prioritise leads. You might use:

- Cold, warm and hot labels
- A numerical score (eg, 1–100)
- Custom categories that make sense for your business

Visualising the sales funnel

CRMs like HighLevel or Pipedrive offer a visual representation of your sales funnel. This might look like:

1. Initial contact
2. Needs assessment

3. Proposal sent

4. Negotiation

5. Closed won/lost

Being able to see at a glance where each lead is sitting in your funnel can help you focus your efforts where they're most needed.

Personalised marketing

By segmenting your leads, you can tailor your marketing efforts. For example: a solar installer could send different information to homeowners versus business owners; an accountant might have separate email campaigns for small business taxes and personal tax returns.

Forms and surveys

One of the most powerful features of modern CRMs is the ability to create custom forms and surveys. This is a lead capture powerhouse; here's how to make the most of it:

Creating custom forms
Design your forms with fields that capture the information most valuable to your business. This might include:

- Basic contact information
- Specific services they're interested in
- Budget range
- Preferred contact method
- Best time to contact

Embed these forms directly into your website or landing pages. This ensures that lead information goes straight into your CRM without any manual data entry.

Smart form strategies
There are a few strategies you can employ to make leads more likely to complete your forms:

- Keep forms short and sweet; ask only for essential information upfront.
- Use dropdown menus or multiple-choice options where possible to make form filling easier.
- Consider using progressive profiling, where returning visitors are asked for new information each time they interact with your site.

Post-submission magic
Here's where you can really shine. After a form is submitted, a step-by-step (automated) process should begin:

1. Set up a redirect after form submission. This should take leads to a 'Thank you' page – but don't stop there!

2. Use this page as an opportunity to:
   - Provide more information about your services
   - Showcase relevant case studies or testimonials
   - Offer a downloadable resource (eg, '10 things to know before installing solar panels')
   - Include a calendar tool for booking a consultation

By doing this, you're not just capturing lead information – you're immediately providing value and moving them further down your sales funnel. Of course, once you have captured your leads, you're only just getting started – next you need to cultivate them so that they progress seamlessly down the funnel and, ultimately, become customers.

> For exclusive *Leads Machine* tools and resources visit: https://francisrodino.com/tools

8
Accelerator 5: Cultivate – Nurture Relationships for Lifelong Wins

It's time now to dive into the art of 'cultivating' leads – turning those first connections into solid business relationships. Here, we're putting to use everything we've learned about our customers and stored in our CRM. Why bother? Simple: it massively increases your chances of making a sale.

In this chapter, we'll walk through the sales funnel, looking at how to use customer insights and CRM systems to nurture leads at each stage. By understanding what makes your potential clients tick, you can tailor your approach, boost conversion rates and build better sales opportunities. From first contact to closing the deal, we'll explore ways to engage and convert leads into loyal customers. By the end, you'll have the tools to turn your sales approach into a well-tended garden of business relationships.

LEADS MACHINE

Have a think about the way you currently cultivate relationships:

How effectively does your system automatically warm and nurture leads around the clock, so that they get to know, like and trust your brand?

1	2	3	4	5	6	7	8	9	10
Lost Opportunities			**Inconsistent at Best**			**Top Class Nurture**		
'We don't nurture leads at all.'			'We're still missing out on 60% of the market.'			'We build meaningful customer relationships and drive leads through our funnel seamlessly on autopilot.'		

If you don't have a system to nurture leads and are not sure where to start, don't worry – automated systems can make the process of cultivating leads pretty simple, and I'm here to walk you through it.

When we built our sales funnel, we broke down the customer journey from a psychological perspective. Now that we know these different stages exist, it's clear we need to approach people and cultivate our relationship with them step by step, tweaking our strategy as we go.

The numbers tell a compelling story. Did you know that 80% of sales are made between the fifth and twelfth contact? Yet, shockingly, 44% of salespeople give up after just one attempt.[13] Talk about leaving money on the table!

Here's another eye-opener: at any given time, only 3% of your market is actively buying. But don't let that discourage you – 40% are poised to begin.[14] That's where cultivation comes in. By following up consistently, you're there when your prospects are ready to buy.

Your competitive edge: Speed to lead

So consistent nurturing is key, but I want to take a moment to zero in on something that can make or break your sales game: speed to lead.

A study by Jay Baer called 'The Time to Win' revealed some pretty eye-opening stats on how much speed really matters when it comes to increasing your sales conversions.[15] For example:

- About two-thirds of customers think speed of response is just as important as price.

---

13 Saleslion, '44% of salespeople give up after one follow-up call' (2022), https://saleslion.io/sales-statistics/44-of-salespeople-give-up-after-one-follow-up-call, accessed 13 November 2024
14 E Burdett, '31 Must-know sales follow-up statistics for 2024 success' (Peak Sales Recruiting, 21 December 2023), www.peaksalesrecruiting.com/blog/sales-follow-up-statistics, accessed 13 November 2024
15 J Baer, *The Time to Win: How to exceed your customers' need for speed* (Ursus 10 Media, 2023)

- More than half of the people in the study (53%) went with the first business to get back to them, even if it cost more.

That second stat is the real kicker – more than half of people went with the first business that got back to them. This means that being quick isn't just about good service, it's about being first to reach the customer – before your competition even has a chance to say 'Hello.'

Did you know that if you follow up with a lead within five minutes, you're nine times more likely to convert them? And supporting Baer's research, a study by Google also found that 30–50% of sales go to the vendor who responds first.[16] I'm always surprised when I speak to service business owners and ask them how long it takes them to get back to an enquiry, and 90% of them say within one to two days. Sadly, that lead will have gone cold by then (especially if you're investing into paid advertising).

All of this means that, if you're not responding to customers immediately, you are literally handing them over to your competitors. But it's not just about being fast with that first response. This applies right the way through the funnel. In this digital age where people are used to having everything in an instant, buyer behaviour has radically changed. People are expecting things to be faster and faster all the time, so if you want

---

16 The Marketing Leadership Council in partnership with Google, *The Digital Evolution in B2B Marketing* (CEB, 2012), www.thinkwithgoogle.com/_qs/documents/677/the-digital-evolution-in-b2b-marketing_research-studies.pdf, accessed October 2024

to stand out and seal the deal, your whole follow-up game needs to be on point, from start to finish.

An interesting fact: it turns out that Baby Boomers are actually the least patient bunch, while Gen-Z is pretty chilled about waiting.[17] Who'd have thought, right? It just goes to show, you've got to know who you're dealing with.

Bottom line? Speed isn't just about good service – it's about putting cash in the bank. People are willing to fork over about 19% more for fast, efficient service.[18] This means that by being speedy with your lead follow-ups, you're not just more likely to land the sale – you might even be able to charge more for it.

So while it might feel like you're pestering people, remember this: persistent, strategic follow-ups are the key to turning prospects into customers. It's not about being pushy – it's about being present and helpful when your potential customers are ready to make a move.

Your 'Zero Moment of Truth'

Let's take a quick moment to acknowledge the phenomenon of the Zero Moment of Truth (ZMOT). This term was coined by Google's Jim Lecinski in

---

17 P Grieve, 'Millennials vs. Gen Z: How their customer service expectations compare', *ZenDesk Blog* (22 April 2021), www.zendesk.co.uk/blog/millennials-vs-gen-z-customer-service-expectations-compare, accessed 13 November 2024

18 S Hyken, 'Today's customer has a need for speed', *Forbes* (8 January 2023), www.forbes.com/sites/shephyken/2023/01/08/todays-customer-has-a-need-for-speed, accessed October 2024

2011 off the back of an extensive research study, and it's changed how we think about customer interactions.[19]

The ZMOT study focuses on the time when a potential customer starts researching a product before they actually buy it. These days, people don't just walk into a shop and make a purchase on the spot. They do their homework first.

How many times does someone interact with a brand before they decide to buy? Well, it's not a fixed number; it can vary quite a bit depending on what's being sold, which industry it's in and even the individual shopper's habits. But the ZMOT study suggests that, on average, people typically engage with about seven to eleven touchpoints before they make up their minds to buy or not. These touchpoints could be anything from reading online reviews and scrolling through social media, to getting marketing emails, comparing products on different websites, checking out online reviews and testimonials, watching videos about the product or even chatting directly with the brand.

With so much information available instantly online, shoppers are more likely than ever to check out multiple sources of information before they decide to buy. This highlights just how important it is for brands to have a strong and consistent presence across various channels. You never know where your potential customer might bump into your brand next!

---

19   J Lecinski, *Winning the Zero Moment of Truth* (Google, 2011)

ACCELERATOR 5: CULTIVATE

Why is this important? Because having a consistent, searchable, online presence is not only going to help your lead nurture system be more effective and profitable, it's going to help you stand out as the first, most desirable service business in your market.

This is why managing your online presence is important. You need to consider how you appear in digital spaces. Lead cultivation starts at this 'zero' point, or moment, when someone first encounters your brand online.

In today's digital world, making a good first impression online matters. But understanding ZMOT is just the start. There are three more stages of lead cultivation that follow, which we'll cover next.

Lead nurture stages

As with growing anything, there are steps to follow when cultivating leads, each with their own activities and workflows. I've discussed the ZMOT, which suggests that you need to think carefully about what leads see and perceive *before* they interact with you. After that, you can break follow-up down into immediate, medium and long-term actions.

Immediate follow-up (speed to lead maximiser)

Right after someone shows interest, it's crucial to have an automatic system that responds straight away. This often happens when someone fills out a form on your landing page, maybe asking for a free guide or some other tempting offer. The goal here is to keep them engaged and encourage them to take the next step.

You'd be surprised how often people fill out an online form and then… nothing. They might get cold feet, life might get in the way or they simply forget. A quick follow-up acts as a gentle nudge, reminding them why they were interested in the first place. This can really boost your conversion rates.

One key rule: always respond on the same platform they used to contact you. If they reached out via Facebook, slide into their Facebook Messenger. If it was via your SMS or WhatsApp website chat widget, keep it to SMS or WhatsApp. It's all about meeting your prospects and customers where they are, making the whole process as smooth as possible.

Medium-term follow-up

If you don't hear back right away, it's time to move those leads into a medium-term follow-up plan. This might involve sending a message every few days.

Here are some scripts for what you might say:

- 'We noticed you were after a quote, but we haven't managed to connect yet. Can we still assist you?'

- 'Just checking if you're still interested – we've actually got a special offer running right now, would you be interested in some information?'

- 'If you've got any questions about our product, we'd be happy to arrange a free demo for you. Would you like me to set that up for you?'

I like to end all of my follow-ups with a question – remember, our primary goal here is to illicit a response.

For service businesses selling high-value items like solar panel installations, setting up an automated system to keep in touch with leads is a no-brainer. Think about it – this is essentially a numbers game, and having an automated system that works twenty-four-seven in the background could produce a handful of extra clients per month. How much more revenue do you think you could generate every year?

Long-term nurture

The reality is that unless it is an emergency, most people aren't necessarily ready to hire you or purchase your services when they enquire for the first time. They might be considering a change, just doing some research or thinking about investing in your expertise, but are not quite ready to buy. For these leads, a long-term nurturing strategy is essential. This could mean sending them a message every week for a year until they're ready to engage your services.

Remember, successful long-term follow-up for service businesses isn't about constantly pushing your services. Instead, it should be a blend of valuable insights, educational content and relevant information about your offerings. Share case studies and client testimonials to showcase your expertise; this will position you as a trusted advisor and authority in your field. The goal here is to instil trust and confidence in your business and help people make a buying decision.

The aim of long-term nurturing is to keep your service at the forefront of your lead's mind. By appearing regularly in their inbox or on their phone, you'll become a familiar and trusted name. When they're finally ready to hire, you'll be their go-to choice.

For this long-term approach, you should use a variety of contact methods. Digital channels and SMS work well for service businesses, but don't discount traditional post. Sending valuable content through the letterbox can be surprisingly effective.

> **PRO TIP**
>
> 'Lumpy' mail – perhaps containing a small, branded item or a well-designed brochure – tends to get opened more often than flat envelopes, which might be mistaken for junk mail.

Lead cultivation in action

Imagine you are a small plumbing and heating company advertising boiler installations on Google. You have been through the value stack exercise from

ACCELERATOR 5: CULTIVATE

earlier in the book and have created an irresistible offer including a free Hive thermostat and a twelve-month free servicing plan with a boiler. Your boilers are supplied with a ten-year warranty to provide total peace of mind.

A person, spotting this offer, clicks on the ad, which takes them to a clear optimised landing page. The call to action is to complete a form to request a quote, share contact details and, as a bonus, get themselves a free guide that you've published, titled 'How to choose the best boiler for the right price'.

That person immediately becomes a lead and, whatever time of day it is that they click on your ad, they automatically go into your CRM database. Your lead then gets an immediate SMS text message from you confirming their request, reassuring them that an engineer will reach out as soon as possible and they'll be able to discuss their quote. This is your immediate follow-up.

The next morning, your lead gets an email, as promised, including your free guide to check out but also encouragement to watch a video where you introduce yourself talking very briefly about how you're a local business committed to supporting local residents. This is your medium-term follow-up. Remember, all of this is happening automatically. You haven't had to do anything. The difference between doing this for 100 customers and 10,000 customers is minimal.

Now imagine when the engineer calls… there's no answer. There's still no answer after three or four attempts. In most cases, that would be the end of their journey.

What if, as part of your cultivation workflow, you send a text message to your lead to ask them if they're still interested, because you have a special offer running at the moment? This is adding an incentive to your medium-term follow-up. If they reply yes, you can automatically connect them with a sales engineer who can discuss their requirements and send them a quote. Now imagine you don't get a reply to the quote. The lead goes quiet. Is the deal over?

Not at all. Your lead can then go into your long-term follow-up workflow and receive weekly emails. Your goal shouldn't be about closing the deal, but helping them to learn more about the specific boiler that's right for their unique situation. You can, over time, advise them on ways they can save money on their energy bills and more.

Eventually, you might send another text message asking them if they're still looking for a boiler installation or if they've found a solution elsewhere. You might get a reply that says no, they haven't gone elsewhere. In fact, they lost the quote, could you resend it? The cycle starts again.

The point of this example is to show that selling your product or service will take multiple touchpoints and outreaches before your leads are ready to say yes because psychologically, they're not necessarily always in the right state of mind to buy. Your job is to be at the forefront of their mind until they do.

The old way vs the new way

The old way of running a business involved keeping emails and contact details in your email system or as contacts in your phone. Do you remember business cards? You might have exchanged them at events and left them on your desk. You might even have scribbled your details on scraps of paper. If things in your business are still old school and all over the place, this will be limiting your ability to grow.

The new world and approach I am advocating gives you the ability to automate the entire process of capturing and cultivating leads. Once you've invested the time and effort in setting them up, they can operate happily without intervention, saving you hours to put into other areas of your business. Embracing this is a key step in preparing your business to scale upwards.

The power of digital assets

Effective lead nurturing is so much easier when you have a compelling reason to reach out to potential customers. The key here is to add value, educate and build a connection with prospects so they come to know, like and trust your brand or business. It's crucial to avoid the pitfall of constant 'sell, sell, sell' messaging. Instead, again we want to focus on creating content that genuinely benefits your prospects, enhances their understanding and positions your business as a trusted resource.

What is a digital asset?

A digital asset is anything that provides value to your audience online while acting as leverage for your business, much like real estate or stocks and shares. Just as these traditional assets work for you by generating income and increasing in value, a digital asset is a powerful online tool or piece of content that works tirelessly to attract, engage and capture potential customers. It generates visibility, educates prospects and helps grow your business and make you money – all without requiring constant manual effort.

Think of your content as an 'ecosystem of assets' that nourishes your lead cultivation workflows with a steady stream of valuable insights. Imagine crafting weekly emails for an entire year – that's fifty-two opportunities to engage with your audience. What could you include in this content ecosystem? Here are some ideas to get you started:

- Informative product guides
- Insightful cost comparisons
- Eye-catching infographics
- Engaging video demonstrations
- Thought-provoking podcasts
- Helpful blogs and vlogs
- In-depth reports and whitepapers

ACCELERATOR 5: CULTIVATE

- Cutting-edge industry research
- Interactive webinars and virtual events
- Engaging social media content
- Educational YouTube videos
- Practical tutorials and 'how-to' guides
- Complimentary training sessions
- Timely news articles and industry updates

The list is probably longer than the above and, of course, you'll be able to think of specific examples for your business. What's important is that by consistently delivering this type of valuable content you're building relationships and establishing your brand as an authority in your field. Keeping your content ecosystem alive and refreshed is a key part of successful lead cultivation practice.

At this point, we've covered how to nurture your leads without coming across like that overly enthusiastic friend who won't stop texting. It's all about cultivating relationships with your potential customers, giving them valuable content and becoming their go-to source of wisdom in your field. Again, think of it as dating, but for business – you're wooing your leads with charming emails and irresistible information, not roses and chocolates.

We've also talked about setting up a system that does all this automatically, so you can, (in the words of one of our clients) 'sit back and watch your profits roll in!' But despite a database full of lucrative leads and leads nurture system in place that means your business is cultivating relationships and conversations all the time, you can still fall at the final hurdle. Now we need to focus our attention on converting those leads into lucrative clients and customers. You need to persuade them to buy.

In the next chapter, we're diving into the art of conversion. We'll be looking at how to turn those flirty glances into full-blown commitments (aka sales). We'll be analysing the key dials and metrics you need to turn to maximise your sales conversions and profit.

So here we go – let's make some sales!

> **For exclusive *Leads Machine* tools and resources visit: https://francisrodino.com/tools**

9
Accelerator 6: Convert – Build An Autopilot System To Close Sales

Let's talk about turning those leads into cold, hard cash. If you've been capturing leads and nurturing them over time, you might have thousands of contacts in your CRM database who know, like and trust your brand. That's brilliant, but nurturing them will only get you so far.

The next crucial question is: how are you going to get these potential customers to take action and actually buy? The answer to this question is what you will take away from this chapter. But before we get started, let's quickly assess your current performance.

LEADS MACHINE

On a scale of one to ten, how effectively does your system automate lead conversions to drive consistent revenue growth by turning prospects into customers effortlessly?

1	2	3	4	5	6	7	8	9	10
Manual and Slow			**More to Go**				**Seamlessly Sophisticated**		
'Automation? We're using spreadsheets and paper.'			'Some basic automations in place, but still need humans to chase leads.'				'Fully automated from end-to-end, no manual intervention needed.'		

Got your number? Great. Whether you're smashing it or struggling, I've got some tricks up my sleeve to help you level up.

In this chapter, I'll be diving into the art and science of converting leads into sales. I'll talk about personalised messaging (because who doesn't love feeling special?), irresistible calls to action and how to create that 'I need this right now!' feeling in your prospects.

We'll also talk numbers – and I promise it won't be as dull as your old maths lessons. We're talking about the metrics that'll help you transform your CRM from a fancy address book into a lean, mean money-making machine.

You should know that improving your conversion rates (or CRO, conversion rate optimisation) isn't a 'set and forget' job. It never ends. I suspect that even if you're doing well, you wouldn't turn down some conversion tips and advice. After all, there's always room for improvement. To help boost your conversion rates, we'll explore the following strategies:

1. Crafting personalised messages for specific opportunities
2. Creating clear and compelling calls to action
3. Harnessing the power of urgency and scarcity
4. Designing seamless checkout and buying experiences
5. Implementing effective tracking metrics and pipeline management

By putting these strategies into practice, you'll be better equipped to guide leads through the conversion process, ultimately driving sales and fuelling your business growth. So let's get cracking on turning those leads into loyal customers!

Personalised follow-ups that close the deal

We're going to kick things off with getting personalisation right. This is not just a buzzword – it's your secret weapon in the conversion game. If you're speaking to the wrong people, nothing in your marketing system will work. It's like trying to sell ice to Inuits – no matter how slick your pitch, you're barking up the wrong tree.

You need to be sending tailored messages to people in your database that address their specific needs. Think about it – if you're a financial adviser, the person who's downloaded your lead magnet on pension planning isn't in the same boat as the newlywed couple looking for help with their tax bill.

Your CRM is your best mate here – use it to segment your audience and create personalised emails and offers. A top-notch CRM will let you provide customised offers, communications or discounts based on past interactions or preferences. Spotted someone clicking on a certain link or accessing specific content on your website? Bingo! You can add them to a segment and hit them with an offer based on that behaviour. It's like being a mind reader, but way less creepy and much more effective.

This personalised approach gives people a more relevant experience with your brand. And let's face it, we all love feeling like a VIP, don't we? But here's the kicker – personalisation alone won't seal the deal. You need to pair it with clear calls to action.

Calls to action

The second strategy for boosting lead conversion is using clear and compelling calls to action (CTAs). I've seen many businesses fall into the trap of sending endless emails without any CTA. They forget to actually ask people to do something. While that's fine for raising awareness, it won't do much for your conversion rates. Remember: if you don't ask, you don't get.

In order to make sales, you need to make offers. The more offers you make, the more sales you'll get. This

ACCELERATOR 6: CONVERT

doesn't always mean asking for a purchase straight away (as we discussed in the cultivation chapter). It could be inviting them to book a free consultation, claim a discount or take any other small step towards engaging with your product or service. The key is to always suggest a clear next step.

Your CTAs should be direct and eye-catching. Place them strategically in your emails, perhaps at the bottom or as a 'PS' after your signature. We all tend to read postscripts, even if we've skimmed the main content. Make it easy for your leads to take that next step towards becoming customers.

For example:

- 'PS: Don't miss out on our limited-time offer! Click here to get 20% off your first purchase.'

- 'PS: We'd love to hear from you! Reply to this email with your feedback for a chance to win a gift card.'

- 'PS: Join our VIP club today and enjoy exclusive discounts and early access to new products. Sign up now!'

- 'PS: Time is running out! Reserve your spot for our upcoming webinar by clicking here. Space is limited!'

- 'PS: Have questions? Our support team is here to help. Contact us now for personalised assistance and tips.'

Don't forget to include CTAs on your website, landing pages, lead magnets, YouTube videos – everywhere. If you send leads to your website without a clear CTA, they're unlikely to take the next step on their own. Without a link to learn more, subscribe or buy now, most prospective customers will simply move on.

As the business owner, it's your job to guide users towards the action you want them to take. Be crystal clear about what you want people to do as they engage with your content, and don't be afraid to repeat your message. Remember, only a small percentage of people will actually open your messages or consume your content in the first place.

Your automated system should consistently send messages, make offers and ask for sales. Strike a balance between educational content and promotional material that reminds people of the opportunity to buy from you. The key is to include a clear, compelling CTA at every touchpoint. No exceptions. By being persistent and consistent with your CTAs, you're increasing the chances that your message will reach and resonate with your audience, ultimately driving more conversions.

Urgency and scarcity: The psychology of action

Next up, let's talk about using urgency and scarcity to convert leads. We touched on this earlier in the book when discussing our second messaging accelerator.

By incorporating 'urgent' and 'scarce' offers into your marketing communications, you create a sense of immediacy that encourages people to act quickly. It's about tapping into that fear of missing out (FOMO) that we all experience.

Urgency relates to time-sensitive offers, like a forty-eight-hour flash sale or a 'deal ends tonight' promotion. Scarcity, on the other hand, is about limited availability – think 'only ten spots left' or 'while stocks last'.

These techniques can be incredibly effective at pushing leads to make a decision. Just remember to keep it genuine – people can spot fake urgency or scarcity a mile off. The goal isn't to pressure people, but to give them a compelling reason to act now rather than later. When done right, creating a sense of urgency and/or scarcity can significantly boost your conversion rates.

Here are some examples for different service businesses:

- For a consulting firm: 'Book your strategy session this week and get a free market analysis report (worth $500)!'

- For a personal trainer: 'Only five spots left in our 12-week body transformation programme – enrol now!'

- For a web design agency: 'First ten clients to sign up get a free year of website maintenance.'

- For a dental practice: 'Book your check-up this month and receive a complimentary tooth whitening treatment.'
- For a financial adviser: 'Tax season special: Get your returns filed by 1 April and save 20% on our services.'

Remember, the key to effectively using urgency and scarcity as conversion accelerators is to strike a delicate balance. It's all about creating a sense of opportunity without coming across as 'salesy' or insincere. Your offers should be genuinely valuable to your prospects and clients.

When you do this right, you'll not only boost your conversion rates but also build trust with your audience. They'll come to see your limited-time offers as opportunities they won't want to miss, rather than high-pressure sales tactics. Try experimenting with different approaches and see what resonates best with your specific audience.

Seamless buying experiences

Once you've prompted potential clients to act, it's crucial to make the conversion process (closing the sale) as smooth as possible. Remember how we talked about speed providing a competitive advantage? In today's fast-paced world, clients want quick and easy solutions.

ACCELERATOR 6: CONVERT

For service businesses, this might mean:

- Making it simple to book a consultation or initial appointment
- Offering an easy-to-use online booking system
- Providing clear, upfront pricing information
- Streamlining your onboarding process

The fewer hurdles that clients need to jump, the more likely they are to follow through. To smooth the path, consider implementing:

- A comprehensive FAQ page to address common queries (it's a great idea to use video to answer the FAQs, which builds rapport and trust)
- Client testimonials and case studies for social proof
- An AI chatbot for instant responses to queries

For ongoing services or retainer-based work, make sure your payment process is hassle-free. Offer various options like direct debit, credit cards or even cryptocurrency if appropriate for your client base. Consider flexible payment plans for higher-ticket services.

Remember, the goal is to make working with or buying from you feel effortless. When it's easy to say yes, more potential customers will become paying customers, and in the service industry, a smooth start often leads to long-term, profitable relationships.

Metrics matter: Measure what drives success

Let's get real for a moment. How well do you know your numbers? I'm not just talking about your bank balance. I'm talking about the metrics that can make or break your service business.

As a service business owner, you might be thinking, 'I don't need all these fancy metrics. I know my business.' You may have been in business for two decades, riding the wave of referrals and word of mouth, and that's a great thing! But if you're looking to break through a plateau and advertise online, knowing your numbers is paramount.

Without solid numbers, you're flying blind. And in today's competitive market, that's a risky game to play. Instead, use metrics to unlock the power of your business data.

METRICS CHEAT SHEET

1. TOTAL SPENT _____
2. NUMBER OF LEADS _____
3. COST PER LEAD _____
4. NUMBER OF SALES _____
5. COST PER SALE _____
6. REVENUE _____
7. REVENUE − SPEND (PROFIT) _____

ACCELERATOR 6: CONVERT

Let's start with the basics:

1. **Total Leads:** How many potential clients are knocking on your door each month? Whether it's via your website, phone calls or walk-ins, you need to know this number. It's also helpful to know where these leads are coming from? Is it your Google Ads? Your networking events? Referrals? Knowing this helps you focus your efforts (and budget) where it counts.

2. **Lead Quality:** Not all leads are created equal. That tyre-kicker who's 'just browsing' isn't the same as the client who's ready to sign on the dotted line. Score your leads based on how likely they are to convert.

3. **Conversion Rate:** This is the big one. What percentage of your leads turn into paying clients? If you're talking to 100 potential clients a month but only landing two jobs, that's a 2% conversion rate. Sound low? It might be time to revisit your sales process (and put in place some of the strategies in this chapter to increase your conversion rate).

4. **Time to Conversion:** How long does it take from first contact to closing the deal? If it's taking months to convert a lead, you might need to streamline your process.

5. **Average Deal Size:** How much does the average client spend with you? This is crucial for forecasting and setting goals.

6. **Cost Per Acquisition (CPA):** How much are you spending to land each new client? This includes your marketing spend, the time you spend on sales calls, everything. If your CPA is higher than your average deal size, you've got a problem.

7. **Customer/Client Lifetime Value (CLV):** How much is a client worth to you over the long haul? For a wedding planner, this might be a one-time deal. For an accountant or a gym owner, it could be years of recurring revenue.

8. **Pipeline Value:** This is the total potential revenue from all active opportunities in your CRM. It gives you a glimpse into future revenue.

Now you might be thinking, 'Francis, this sounds like a lot of work.' And you're right, it does take some effort to track these numbers. But once you know them, you can make informed decisions that will skyrocket your business.

Let's say you're a personal trainer. You know that your average client stays with you for six months and pays $200 a month. That's a CLV of $1,200. Suddenly, spending $300 on Facebook ads to land a new client doesn't seem so scary, does it?

Or maybe you're a web designer. You notice that leads from referrals convert at 50%, while leads from

ACCELERATOR 6: CONVERT

your Google Ads only convert at 5%. Might be time to double down on that referral programme, right?

The beauty of a good CRM system is that it can track most of these numbers for you automatically. No more late nights with a calculator and a spreadsheet. But you can't improve what you don't measure, so start measuring, start improving and watch your conversion rates soar.

Next up, we'll look at how to use these numbers to refine your sales process and turn more of those leads into happy, paying clients.

The sales pipeline: Track, manage, convert

Alright, we've set up a slick system to convert leads into paying customers and everything is being measured. But how do we know if it's actually working? This is where tracking metrics and managing your pipeline come into play. Don't worry, it's not as daunting as it sounds – and it's absolutely crucial for your business's success.

Your CRM system should make tracking these metrics a breeze. HighLevel, for example, gives you a visual representation of your entire pipeline. You can see at a glance how many leads are in each stage of your sales funnel and the potential revenue they represent.

LEADS MACHINE

YOUR SALES PIPELINE

NEW LEAD	IN CONTACT	FOLLOW UP	SALES CALL
			WON!
			WON!

Why does this matter? We're not just collecting data for the sake of it – it's about using it to make decisions. Let's say you notice you have lots of leads in the 'awareness' stage, but very few moving to 'consideration'. This might indicate that your initial follow-up needs work. Or maybe you see that leads from referrals convert at a much higher rate than those from Google Ads. That's valuable intel for your marketing strategy.

Here are some ways to put your metrics to work:

- **Identify bottlenecks:** Where are leads getting stuck in your pipeline? Is there a particular stage where you're losing a lot of potential customers? Focus your efforts on improving that stage.

- **Optimise your marketing spend:** If certain lead sources are converting better than others, consider allocating more of your budget there.

- **Personalise your approach:** Use the data in your CRM to tailor your communication. If you know a lead has been stuck in the 'consideration' stage for a while, maybe it's time for a special offer to nudge them towards making a decision.

- **Set realistic goals:** Understanding your conversion rates and average deal size allows you to set achievable targets for your business.

- **Forecast revenue:** With a clear view of your pipeline, you can make more accurate predictions about future income. This is invaluable for budgeting and planning.

Remember, the goal isn't to obsess over every slight fluctuation in your metrics. It's to get a clear, data-driven picture of your sales process so you can make informed decisions.

> **PRO TIP**
>
> Don't just look at these numbers in isolation. Compare them month over month, quarter over quarter. Are you seeing improvements? If not, it's time to dig deeper and figure out why.

By consistently tracking and analysing these metrics, you're not just guessing at what works – you *know* what works. And in the competitive world of service businesses, that knowledge is power.

The Ninja trick to explosive business growth: Weekly LAPS

When it comes to scaling your business, it's not the flashy, high-profile stuff you see online that will be most effective. The big launch events, the massive social media campaigns, the public-facing spectacle – those are just the tip of the iceberg. They succeed because of something far less glamorous yet infinitely more powerful happening behind the scenes.

The true growth engine is a weekly commitment to the LAPS process: Leads, Appointments, Presentations and Sales. This approach, inspired by one of my mentors, the entrepreneur and influencer Daniel Priestley, has been a cornerstone in every business I've scaled from zero to a million dollars within the first year.

Priestley's concept of LAPS is straightforward yet transformative: by breaking down your growth into these four measurable stages, you gain laser-sharp focus on what actually drives revenue.[20] More importantly, when you know your conversion

---

20 D Priestley, 'Every business should have a sales process...' [LinkedIn post] (2024), www.linkedin.com/posts/danielpriestley_sales-salesprocess-salespresentation-activity-7158386675323133954-Yfyn, accessed January 2025

numbers at each step, you unlock the ability to fine-tune your business engine with precision.

Think of it this way: every time you focus on LAPS, you're adding strength to each link in your sales chain. Leads are the potential customers; appointments get you in front of those leads; presentations are where you showcase your value; and sales close the deal. If any one of these links is weak, the whole chain suffers.

Every week, without fail, we dive into our LAPS dashboard. This habit keeps us anchored to the numbers that matter most, from lead volume to close rates. It's a rhythmic review, and it pushes us to optimise each part of the sales funnel. Our team knows that when they focus on LAPS, they're fuelling growth. And the numbers speak for themselves.

The power of knowing your numbers

Here's where the real ninja trick comes into play: when you know your conversion numbers, you're able to tweak each dial – leads, appointments, presentations and sales – to create predictable growth. It's a feedback loop of data-driven adjustments. If leads are down, we know we need to ramp up outreach or experiment with a new audience segment. If appointments are lagging, we optimise our booking system or fine-tune our message. Each tweak compounds, creating a powerful momentum over time.

So if you want a business that doesn't just grow but takes off, forget the grand gestures. Focus on relentless weekly execution, drilling down into each part of the LAPS process. Those big campaigns will work, but only because you've built a solid, scalable engine behind them.

Automation and AI: Your 24/7 sales team

In the world of modern business, the line between science fiction and reality is blurrier than ever. The rise of automation and AI has opened up possibilities that seemed far-fetched just a few years ago. For service business owners, this technological revolution is potentially transformative, if you embrace it.

Imagine having a sales team that never sleeps, never takes a holiday and never misses an opportunity. That's the promise of automation and AI. But don't worry, we're not talking about replacing your staff with an army of robots. This is about augmenting your human touch with digital efficiency.

The beauty of these tools lies in their ability to handle the repetitive tasks that eat up your time. Take follow-ups, for instance. We all know the importance of responding quickly to enquiries, but let's face it – you can't be glued to your inbox twenty-four-seven. That's where automated follow-ups come in. Within seconds of a potential client reaching out, they can receive a personalised response, complete with helpful information and next steps. All of this happens without a human being lifting a finger.

ACCELERATOR 6: CONVERT

But it doesn't stop there. The real magic happens when you start to nurture your leads over time. Drip campaigns, a series of automated emails, can keep your business front of mind without you having to remember to hit 'send'. It's like planting seeds and watching them grow, except these seeds are potential clients, and they're being watered with valuable, relevant content.

Then there's the rise of AI chatbots. These digital conversationalists are becoming increasingly sophisticated, capable of handling initial enquiries, qualifying leads and even booking appointments. Imagine waking up to find your digital assistant has filled your diary with qualified prospects while you were catching up on your beauty sleep.

The real power of these tools lies not just in their efficiency, but in their ability to personalise at scale. By tapping into the wealth of data stored in your CRM, you can create experiences that feel tailor-made for each client. It's like having a photographic memory for every interaction, preference and need of your entire client base.

It's important to stress that this isn't about replacing the human element of your business. Far from it. It's about enhancing it. By automating the routine stuff, you free up time and mental space for what really matters: building relationships, solving complex problems and delivering exceptional service.

The best part? You don't need to be a tech wizard to harness this power. Modern CRM systems have made these tools accessible to businesses of all sizes. You can start small, perhaps with a simple automated follow-up sequence, and build from there. As you get more comfortable, you can add layers of sophistication, creating a system that's as unique as your business.

In the end, automation and AI are simply tools – incredibly powerful tools, but tools nonetheless. They're there to serve you, to make your life easier and your business more profitable. Used wisely, they can be the secret ingredient that takes your service business from good to great, from struggling to thriving.

So, as we stand on the brink of this new era, the question isn't whether you can afford to embrace these technologies. The question is: can you afford not to?

> **For exclusive** *Leads Machine* **tools and resources,** visit https://francisrodino.com/tools

PART FOUR
DRIVE: FROM INVISIBLE TO IRRESISTIBLE

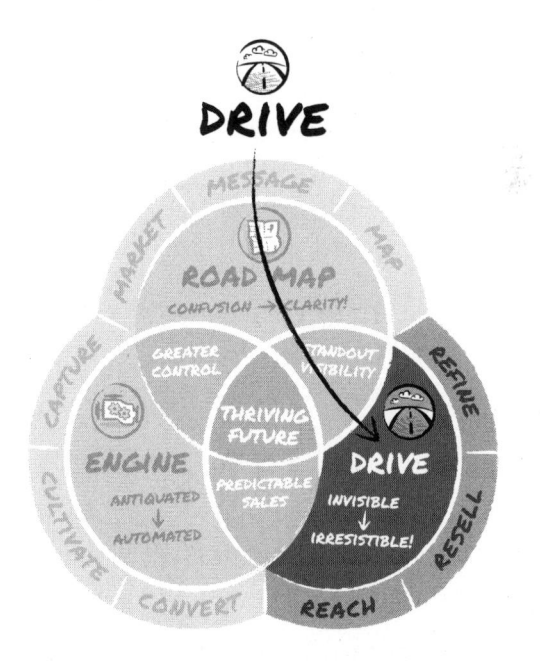

In the world of business, we often hear the term 'scale' as a catch-all for 'grow and profit'. But when it comes to scaling a service business, the concept goes beyond size and revenue – it's about momentum, direction and impact. This section, Drive, is where we focus on accelerating your business forward by reaching new clients, reselling to your current ones and refining your marketing engine to keep things running smoothly. Through years of helping hundreds of businesses grow with automated marketing systems, I've learned that scaling a service business boils down to three core drivers for success:

1. **Reach – Reach More People, Make A Bigger Impact.** Expanding your brand's presence to consistently attract new potential clients and deepen engagement

2. **Resell – Turn Customers Into Raving Fans And Repeat Buyers.** Fostering loyalty by engaging existing clients to use more of your services, maximising retention and lifetime value

3. **Refine – Optimise Your Marketing For Lasting Success.** Continuously optimising your approach, adjusting strategies and enhancing efficiency to ensure peak performance

For the purpose of this book, I'm not going to be talking about hiring more people, adding new services, or moving to a bigger office (although you might very well have to consider all these things as you grow).

As a small business, the goal here is maximum profit with minimum overhead; fortunately, in this day and age we have all the tools we need readily available and accessible.

Everything we're going to cover in this last part of the book is focused on making more money, not spending it. It's about being clever with your resources and using digital tools and strategies to grow your service business without breaking the bank.

For service businesses, this way of scaling is a game-changer. It lets you bring in more clients and cash without having to work yourself into the ground or spend a fortune. It's about getting the most out of every client relationship and fine-tuning your marketing to bring in a steady stream of new business.

Before we dive in, a disclaimer: scaling a service that's not already working, or unproven in the market, is a risk. It's highly likely that you'll just end up with more mess (and a lot of wasted money). If your fulfilment is inconsistent and your service delivery is slow, or you have to hire more people to onboard clients and deliver your services, trying to scale up will only amplify these issues. It's like turning up the volume on a scratchy record – your problems will just get louder.

You know, this whole scaling business reminds me of my grandma's chocolate cake. Now that was a cake to behold – soft, creamy centre, rich chocolate flavour, absolute perfection every single time. How did she do it? Simple. She had a recipe, and she stuck to it religiously. The right ingredients, precise measurements, proper preparation and spot-on bake time. Follow that recipe, and you'd get that same delicious cake, time after time, without fail. Well, my friends, scaling your service business with paid ads is a bit like that. You need the right ingredients (a solid service offering), precise measurements (knowing your numbers), proper preparation (having your systems in place) and the right 'bake time' (consistent execution). Get all these elements right, and you've got yourself a recipe for success that you can replicate again and again. It's not about making a different cake each time – it's about perfecting your recipe and then using it to serve up success on a larger scale.

CASE STUDY: Scaling one of the UK's most successful home service businesses

One of our clients at Lead Hero AI, a major player in the UK boiler installation and renewables industry with annual revenue of over £15 million, partnered with us to implement our RED Method. The results were remarkable: they doubled their sales in just twelve months, solidifying their position as an industry leader.

Like many trades and home service businesses, our client had been relying on inconsistent, ad-hoc marketing efforts. This approach had left them unable to tap into new markets or maximise value from existing clients. They recognised they were missing out on significant revenue opportunities.

We developed a comprehensive strategy based on the Reach, Resell and Refine accelerators. Then we took it a step further by implementing advanced marketing automation and integrating various systems to streamline their operations.

Reach

We implemented a balanced marketing strategy that combined automated lead generation and paid advertising with organic customer attraction methods to expand visibility.

This included:

- Targeted Google and Facebook ad campaigns
- Improved SEO to boost visibility among homeowners in key areas
- Regular blog updates with valuable home maintenance tips
- Active engagement with local communities on social media

Crucially, we integrated an AI assistant to engage with leads, have initial conversations, qualify prospects and book consultations. This significantly improved the efficiency of their lead generation process.

Resell

We focused on maximising customer value by re-engaging with existing and lapsed leads through:

- Segmented, automated marketing campaigns tailored to different customer groups
- Introduction of a loyalty programme offering discounts and priority scheduling for repeat customers

- Implementation of WhatsApp automation, allowing the entire team to benefit from shared videos, photos and tracked conversations with customers

Refine

We instilled a culture of continuous improvement through optimisation and integration, by:

- Setting up an analytics dashboard to track key performance metrics
- Conducting A/B testing on ads, emails and website landing pages
- Regularly collecting and acting on customer feedback

We also integrated their phone system and sales pipeline into a unified platform to allow seamless tracking of customer interactions across all touchpoints, from initial contact to post-installation follow-ups.

The key outcomes the client saw were:

- Doubled sales in twelve months
- Expanded reach to new customer segments through AI-assisted lead generation
- Increased value from existing customer base via automated, personalised marketing
- Improved team communication and customer interaction tracking through WhatsApp automation
- Enhanced overall efficiency through integrated systems and automation

Our client achieved impressive results without any major operational changes. They simply leveraged advanced automation and integration to replicate their existing, successful sales approach more efficiently and at a larger scale.

This success demonstrates the power of a well-executed, data-driven marketing strategy combined with cutting-edge integrated automation. By focusing on reaching new customers, reselling to existing ones and continuously refining their approach, they were able to scale their business significantly in a relatively short period.

The above case study illustrates how the Reach, Resell and Refine accelerators, when coupled with advanced marketing automation and system integration, can be a powerful tool for scaling service businesses, even in traditional industries like plumbing and heating.

We've seen how this approach can really shake things up for a business, so let's roll up our sleeves and get stuck into the first part of our Drive strategy: Reach.

Ready to learn how to make some noise and turn heads in your industry? Let's dive in and see how we can get your phone ringing off the hook.

10
Accelerator 7: Reach – Reach More People, Make A Bigger Impact

This is where the journey kicks into high gear – the first accelerator of the Drive lever. It's all about hitting the gas on visibility, getting your brand out there and drawing in a steady stream of new customers. Think of it like this: you've got a fantastic service, but if nobody knows about it, you're not going to get very far, are you? That's where 'Reach360 Method' comes in. We're going to look at clever ways to get your business in front of more eyeballs – and not just any eyeballs, but the right ones.

We'll chat about everything from savvy ad strategies to organic growth tricks that won't cost you an arm and a leg. It's not about shouting the loudest, it's about making sure the right people hear you.

LEADS MACHINE

Want to know the quickest way to get your business noticed? It's easy – but you've got to spend some cash. I'm talking about paid online advertising.

Now, I'm not saying there aren't great traditional methods to advertise your business – local newspapers, radio, TV, they all have their place, and depending on your budget, services and target market, those channels might be good options for you. But here we're interested in the methods to grow and scale your business *online*, so we'll be looking primarily at online channels like Google Search ads and social media ads (Facebook, Instagram, LinkedIn etc).

Let's take a moment to acknowledge where we are today. We're living in a pretty amazing era for business. For the first time in history, anyone with a credit card and a decent idea can put their brand in front of thousands, even millions of people, just by clicking a few buttons. Incredible.

Let's talk numbers for a second, because they're pretty mind-blowing. As I'm writing this, Google is handling a whopping 8.5 billion searches every single day.[21] That's not a typo – billion with a 'b'. It's been the go-to for people looking for products and services online for ages now, and for good reason.

But Google's not the only big player in town. Meta's family of apps – that's Facebook, Instagram, WhatsApp and Messenger – are chatting with nearly

---

21 D Chaffey, 'Search engine marketing statistics 2024' (Smart Insights, 1 February 2024), www.smartinsights.com/search-engine-marketing/search-engine-statistics, accessed October 2024

ACCELERATOR 7: REACH

4 billion people every month,[22] with Instagram having 2 billion monthly users scrolling through photos and videos. If you're more of a suit-and-tie type running a B2B company, LinkedIn's got you covered with its 774 million members.[23] That's a lot of potential handshakes and business cards, if you know what I mean.

The best part? All these platforms are right there, waiting for you to jump in. It's like having a megaphone that can reach billions of people – you just need to learn how to use it. And trust me, it's not as complicated as it might seem. What we should *really* be excited about is the fact that our parents didn't have this golden opportunity. For them, the game plan was pretty straightforward – land a job, clock in and out (for decades) and, if they were lucky, maybe they'd scrape together enough for a decent retirement.

Now, whether you're running a small cleaning company or offering IT support, you can compete with big companies without needing a massive budget. In fact, small businesses typically have an advantage; they're leaner, more agile, quicker on their feet – faster to make decisions, iterate and reach new markets. All you need is a laptop and some know-how. If you've got a business or a dream, there's never been a better time to go for it. The tools are there, the audience is

---

22 SJ Dixon, 'Meta Platforms: Statistics and facts' (Statista, 16 February 2024), www.statista.com/topics/9038/meta-platforms/#topicOverview, accessed October 2024
23 R Adamson, 'The power of LinkedIn: Unveiling top 30 LinkedIn statistics' (Charle, 15 January 2024), www.charle.co.uk/articles/linkedin-statistics, accessed October 2024

LEADS MACHINE

waiting – it's an exciting time to be a business owner or entrepreneur.

A quick note on SEO. This is another digital activity that's important in its own right, but I'm not going to cover it in depth here (that's a whole other book). Here's the gist of it though: SEO is playing the long game to climb Google's rankings naturally, while paid ads are like buying a first-class ticket to the top of the search results.

For the purpose of creating consistent, predictable sales, we're focusing on quick wins, which means paid ads. SEO is getting more competitive by the day. It's like a never-ending Formula One race – stop investing in your SEO, and you can fall behind fast. So while SEO is valuable, for the purposes of this book, we're looking at faster, more controllable methods to scale your business.

Let me ask you:

How effectively are you integrating paid advertising to maximise your brand's visibility and drive consistent leads online?

1	2	3	4	5	6	7	8	9	10
Barely Visible			**Somewhat Visible**				**#1 in the Market**		
'Little to no integration of paid and organic methods.'			'Running some ads, but we lack an effective, continuous presence.'				'Our brand is virtually everywhere in our target market, and dominates the digital landscape.'		

Whether you're just starting out or you're already making waves, the strategies we're about to learn can help you take your paid advertising to the next level.

Remember, in the digital world, standing still is the same as moving backwards. So let's get moving!

Using Google and Facebook Ads to scale your business

Having worked with hundreds of service business owners to grow and scale their business online, I know that the most pressing, constant challenge is getting clients predictably and consistently.

But here's the thing – when prospects come to our events, webinars or sales presentations and I ask them, 'What's your advertising budget?', I am often met with blank stares or nervous laughs. It's like many service providers are stuck in this endless cycle of word-of-mouth referrals and cold calling, without ever considering a more proactive approach.

Why? There's this stubborn myth that advertising just doesn't work for service businesses. I hear it all the time: 'Oh, our clients only come through referrals,' or 'Advertising is too expensive for a small operation like ours.' This is especially common among traditional service providers – your local electricians, family law firms, IT support companies and life coaches.

This kind of thinking is one of the biggest roadblocks to scaling your service business and driving it forward.

Digital platforms like Google, Facebook, and Instagram are absolute game-changers for service businesses. They're precision tools that can address your specific challenges. Struggling to fill your appointment book? Tired of feast-or-famine cycles? Want to attract higher-paying clients? Advertising on these platforms can help.

Before we get going, a quick disclaimer: before you even think about scaling with paid advertising, you need to make sure your core business operations are running like a well-oiled machine. Your services should be top-notch, your delivery should be consistent and your clients should be singing your praises. Only then should you consider ramping things up.

If you're a startup, don't have many clients or are unsure about your capability to deliver at scale, your business may not be ready for paid ads. The time to start using paid ads to reach more people is when you've got 'proof of concept' – meaning you've already won a few clients and so you know your offer sells.

Breaking the scroll: How disruptive advertising works

Imagine a potential customer scrolling through their Facebook feed, catching up with their friends and family. They're just mindlessly scrolling, so any ad that wants their attention needs to stand out with a strong hook. This is where disruptive advertising comes in – it grabs attention with a striking visual element, whether that's an image or a video, and has literally only a few seconds to make an impact. Think of pop-up ads on websites or autoplay videos that interrupt YouTube content; they break the flow and, even if just for a moment, 'stop the scroll'.

How Meta (Facebook) makes money

Meta, being a public company, has one primary objective: to make money for its shareholders. They do this by keeping users on their platforms as long as possible, using sophisticated methods to keep them engaged and scrolling – because the longer people stay, the more ads Meta can sell.

For us advertisers, it is better to work with Facebook's algorithm than against it. For example, Facebook supports content with likes, shares and comments because it means people are interacting with it. If your ad is boring, it's not going to get a lot of reach.

If your ad gets a healthy amount of likes and interactions, it will be rewarded with a lower cost. To help you do this, Facebook has developed advanced targeting options based on demographics, geographic location, psychographic data, hobbies and interests. You can use these targeting methods to 'dial into' your market and find people interested in your offer.

People don't ignore ads; they ignore ads that aren't relevant to them.

Imagine you own a boutique fitness studio looking to attract new members. You can use Facebook or Instagram's demographic targeting to reach people between twenty and forty years old who have shown interest in health and fitness. You can also target people who like bodybuilding, for example, or even those who follow Arnold Schwarzenegger. You might create short engaging video ads featuring client testimonials and showing off your studio and its facilities, amenities, equipment and classes. Do this well, and you'll attract people who are already engaging with health-related content on Facebook. You can use geographical targeting to target people within one or two miles of your gym's location, too. In this way, you can get incredibly specific about where you appear and who you want your digital social media ads to reach.

It's fair to say that the more tightly you specify your audience, the more expensive advertising is, as making the net smaller means your cost per lead will increase. With a wider net, you'll get more people, lots of views and a greater number of leads at a lower cost, but the trade-off is they will be less of a good fit to your business.

Understanding campaign types

Every marketing campaign should have a clear objective – it sounds straightforward, but it's crucial to understand campaign objectives so you can set the right goal for optimising your efforts in your digital ads platform. Whether you're aiming to boost brand awareness, drive website traffic or generate leads, your campaign objective will shape how your ads are delivered and to whom. In this section, I'm going to

ACCELERATOR 7: REACH

talk about what campaign objectives are and how to use them.

Now, I'll be using Facebook as the primary example here, but campaign objectives are pretty universal in the digital advertising world. Whether you're advertising on Google, TikTok, LinkedIn, Instagram, YouTube or even some shiny new platform that's popped up since I wrote this (and trust me, that's entirely possible in this fast-paced digital landscape), campaign objectives tell the all-seeing, all-knowing AI algorithm what to optimise your campaign for.

So before you launch your campaign, think about your end goal. What do you want people to do? It's like setting off on a road trip – you need to know where you're going before you start driving, right?

Facebook offers seven main objectives: awareness, traffic, engagement, app install, lead generation, conversion and sales. For service business owners, some of these objectives will resonate more than others. If you're a local plumber, you're probably more interested in lead generation than app installs. A life coach might focus on engagement to build trust, while a boutique law firm might prioritise awareness in their local community. The key is to match your business goals with the right campaign objective, to avoid blindly throwing money at ads and crossing your fingers. It's about being strategic, understanding what each objective can do for your business, and then leveraging that to get the best results.

Whether you're a dog groomer looking to fill up your appointment book, or an IT consultant trying to land more corporate clients, starting with a clear objective is your first step to advertising success. It's all about picking the right tool for the job – and then knowing how to use it. So let's look at some possible campaign objectives and types for service businesses, and how you would go about setting them up.

Reach campaigns

Awareness (otherwise called 'reach') campaigns are a bit like putting up a billboard on a busy highway. The goal? It's all in the name – they are made to reach more people. In other words, to get your brand in front of as many eyeballs as possible.

For small service businesses, especially those needing leads ASAP, these campaigns might not be your immediate go-to strategy. They focus on quantity over quality, casting a wide net rather than targeting people who are ready to buy right now.

In his book *Magnetic Marketing*, Dan Kennedy uses the Goodyear blimp as an example of awareness advertising.[24] Imagine that massive blimp floating over a packed football stadium – impressive, right? It certainly gets the brand in front of thousands of eyeballs (and costs a fortune too), but how many of those fans are actually in the market for new tyres?

---

24 DS Kennedy, *Magnetic Marketing: How to attract a flood of new clients that pay, stay and refer* (Forbes Books, 2018)

ACCELERATOR 7: REACH

It's a vital lesson for service businesses. Awareness campaigns, like that blimp, can indeed put your name out there, but they're not always the most efficient way to generate immediate leads. The trick is to balance broad awareness with targeted strategies that reach people when they actually need your services.

Imagine you run a plumbing business. An awareness campaign might show your logo to thousands of people in your area. Great for getting your name out there, right? But here's the catch – most of those people won't need a plumber at that exact moment. It's not going to immediately make your phone ring off the hook.

However, don't write off awareness and reach campaigns just yet. They play a crucial role in a comprehensive marketing strategy, especially for service businesses looking to build their brand over time. Think of it this way: every time someone scrolls past your ad, it's like they're driving past your billboard. They might not need your services today, but when their boiler breaks down next month, guess whose name might pop into their head?

These kinds of campaigns are about playing the long game. They're great for:

1. New businesses trying to make a splash in their local market

2. Established businesses launching a new service

3. Any service business looking to stay top of mind in their community

The key is to use these campaigns as part of a larger strategy. Combine them with more targeted approaches, and you've got a powerful marketing mix. You're not just fishing for immediate leads; you're cultivating a pool of potential customers who'll think of you and choose you when they need your services.

Remember, in the service business world, being known and trusted is half the battle. Awareness and reach campaigns help you win that battle, even if they don't immediately fill up your appointment book.

Traffic and sales campaigns

If you're looking to send people to a specific online destination (typically outside of the platform you're advertising on, like your website or landing page, even a third-party site), you might use a traffic objective.

These campaigns tend to cost more for a couple of key reasons. Primarily, it's because Facebook's business model revolves around keeping users engaged on their platform. They make their money by selling ads, so their algorithm is designed to keep people scrolling through Facebook. When you're asking to direct users away from the platform, you're essentially working against Facebook's core objective. As a result, they charge a premium for these outbound clicks. It's like asking a shop owner to direct customers to a competitor's store. So they'll do it, but at a higher price. Second, the users who click through are often more qualified leads, showing a higher level of interest in what's being offered.

ACCELERATOR 7: REACH

For service businesses, traffic campaigns can be particularly effective. They allow companies to guide potential clients directly to their online booking systems, contact forms or informational pages. It's a great way to shortcut the customer journey from initial interest to conversion.

However, it's important to note that you shouldn't expect huge numbers of click-throughs. You'll likely need to show your ad to quite a few people to get a meaningful number of clicks, but those who do click are often more likely to turn into actual clients or customers. From my experience, for service businesses, average click-through rates on Facebook range from 0.5% to 1.5%. This means that for every 1,000 people who see your ad, only five to fifteen of them might click on it; you need to factor these metrics into your advertising budget.

While these figures can provide a useful benchmark, it's important to understand that individual campaign performance can vary depending on your ad creative, targeting, the relevance of your offer and your overall campaign strategy. If your CTRs are even higher, then your ads are doing great!

Additionally, CTR isn't the be all and end all of ad performance. In some cases, a lower CTR that attracts higher quality leads can be more valuable than a higher CTR with less interested users. The key is to view CTR in conjunction with your other metrics, such as conversion rate and CPA, to get a true gauge of the effectiveness of your traffic and sales campaigns.

Engagement campaigns

Engagement campaigns are all about getting more people to interact with your content. It could be a social post, a video, an event or maybe even a link to your blog. The goal here is get people talking, liking and sharing your content.

You might use an engagement campaign to boost the buzz around a new product launch, get people excited about an upcoming event or simply to keep your brand at the forefront of people's minds. They're also brilliant for showing social proof – a video testimonial with hundreds of likes and positive comments is the kind of content that can really build trust in your brand.

For example, let's say you own a local physiotherapy clinic. You could run an engagement campaign around a video showing a simple at-home exercise for back pain. As people comment with their experiences or questions and share the video with friends who have similar issues, you're not just increasing engagement – you're positioning your clinic as a helpful authority in your community.

App installs

App install campaigns are a highly specific type of campaign intended to encourage users to download apps from the iOS or Android app stores. They are designed explicitly around video content and can effectively engage people with rich content and drive traffic to product download pages.

Lead generation

Lead generation campaigns on Facebook are designed to collect information from interested users without them having to leave the platform. This means you will typically enjoy a lower cost per lead – albeit at the expense of lead quality.

Here's how they work: Facebook provides an in-platform mini landing page and data capture process called 'lead forms'. You don't need to build anything fancy on your own website or a landing page; it's all right there, seamlessly integrated into the user's Facebook experience.

Lead forms are especially efficient and effective for service businesses. Think about it – you're catching people where they're already spending their time, and you're making it dead easy for them to show interest in what you're offering. Whether you're after newsletter sign-ups, offering free downloads, promoting special offers or building a wait list, these campaigns can do the heavy lifting for you.

For instance, imagine you're a personal trainer. You could run a lead generation campaign offering a 'Free 7-day fat-burning workout plan'. Users can sign up without leaving Facebook, making them much more likely to do it. You get their contact details, they get valuable content and you've opened the door for future communication – all without the friction (and cost) of sending them to an external site.

Overall, Facebook lead generation campaigns offer a smooth, user-friendly way to capture valuable lead information. They're a powerful tool in any service business's digital marketing arsenal, helping you build your customer base with minimal fuss and maximum efficiency.

Conversions/sales

The conversion objective is designed to guide potential clients towards taking that crucial next step in engaging your services. Here, the Facebook algorithm will optimise the campaign to encourage users to take a specific action – whatever that may be.

This can mean more than just making a quick purchase. Take a corporate law firm, for instance. A conversion in this case might be a potential client booking an initial consultation to discuss their legal needs. For a management consultancy, it could be a prospect downloading an in-depth whitepaper and then scheduling a strategy call. Consider a boutique architecture firm; their conversion goal might be getting potential clients to submit project briefs or book a site visit. For a specialised IT services provider, a conversion could be a company signing up for a comprehensive IT audit.

It's important to note that, if you're sending people to your website, to get the most out of these campaigns you'll need to set up some special tracking tools (pixels) on your website or landing pages. These tools will pick up data from your website and send them back to your ad platform, so that data can inform your analytics. It's important to have proper tracking set up for all your campaigns, so you can see what's working and what isn't and make necessary adjustments to improve your results.

Intent-driven advertising – the power of Google Ads

All the examples and campaigns above are 'disruptive', primarily designed to stop people in their tracks by saying 'Look at me!'. They work by catching people's attention when they're doing something else, like scrolling through their social media feed. But there's another approach to online advertising – one that doesn't interrupt your potential customers' scrolling or browsing.

Non-disruptive advertising is more like being in the right place at the right time, when people are searching for your services. They align with what users are already looking for or interested in. Google search ads are a great example of non-disruptive advertising. When someone's looking for a 'plumber near me', and your ad for plumbing services pops up, it's not interrupting them, it's helping them find what they need.

Another type of non-disruptive advertising is 'native' ads. These ads blend in with the content around them; for example, they might look like an article on a news website or a post in your social media feed. They appear as a 'branded' editorial. The idea is to provide information or entertainment that fits naturally with what people are already engaging with.

The beauty of non-disruptive advertising is that it can feel less intrusive to your potential customers. Instead of shouting 'Look at me!' it's more like saying, 'Hey, I see you're interested in this. We might be able to help.' It's about being useful and relevant, rather than just grabbing attention.

With non-disruptive ads, the goal isn't to distract or interrupt, but to be there with the right information when your potential clients are already in a mindset to engage with services like yours.

Google Ads

By far the most popular form of digital non-disruptive advertising is Google Ads, formerly known as Google Ad Words. Google's reach is pretty mind-blowing: every single day, around 8.5 billion searches are punched into that familiar search bar.[25] We're talking about hundreds of millions of people turning to Google for answers, shopping, random facts – all sorts. And if you're looking to get your business on page one of the search results without having to invest the time and money it takes to rank your website organically (months, if not years) – Google Ads are your fast-track ticket.

---

25 Chaffey, 'Search engine marketing statistics 2024'

ACCELERATOR 7: REACH

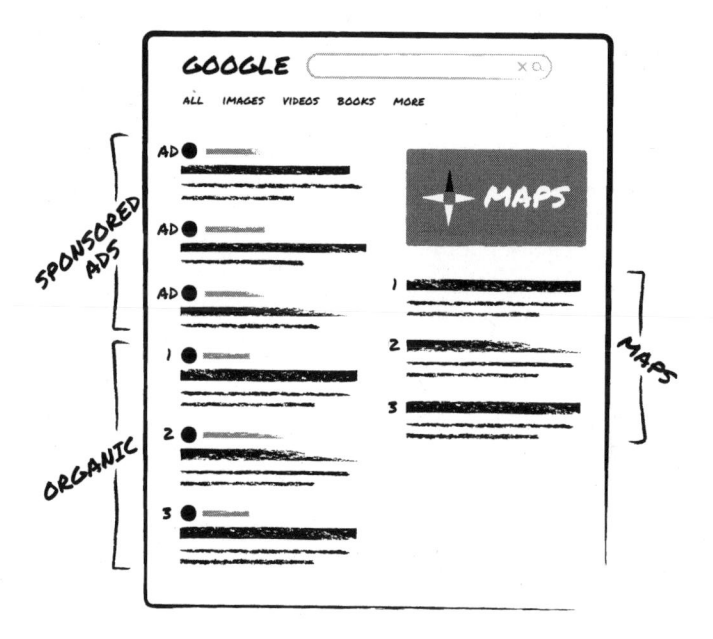

Similar to Facebook, Google's campaigns are designed with specific business outcomes in mind, and they have advertising options for every kind of campaign goal. They've got a massive network that lets you put your ads just about anywhere – search results, websites, videos, mobile apps, you name it. You literally have a smorgasbord of advertising possibilities.

But before you spend any money, as I mentioned before, you need to ask yourself: 'What do I want people to do after they see my ad?' Are you trying to get more people to your website? Boost your sales? Generate some leads? Or just get your brand's name out there?

Google's got seven main types of campaign to choose from:

1. Search
2. Display
3. Shopping
4. Video
5. App
6. Local
7. Performance Max
8. Google Guaranteed

Each has its own strengths, which we'll discuss below, so pick the one that best fits what you're after. It's like having a toolbox full of different tools – you need to choose the right one for the job at hand.

Search

You know those 'sponsored' results you see at the top of your Google search results? Those are Google Search ads, they're those text ads that pop up at the top of Google search results when you're looking for something specific.

Here's why they're so powerful: imagine someone with a burst pipe actively searching for 'emergency plumber in Manchester' at 2am. You're not interrupting

ACCELERATOR 7: REACH

anyone's day – your ad pops up right when they need you most. It's like being in the right place at the right time, every time.

These ads blend in seamlessly with regular search results, so they don't feel intrusive. They're designed to be helpful, answering the searcher's question or solving their problem. It's a win-win – the user finds what they need, and you get a potential customer who's already interested in what you offer.

For service businesses looking for higher quality leads, search ads are brilliant for capturing the 'ready to buy' crowd.

LANDING PAGE

WANT A FREE COPY OF OUR..?

BUY!

$$\frac{\# \text{ CLICKS}}{\# \text{ LEADS}} = \% \text{ LEADS}$$

$$\frac{\text{AMOUNT SPENT}}{\# \text{ LEADS}} = \text{CPL}$$

Display ads

Display ads are like digital billboards scattered across the internet. They appear on millions of websites in Google's digital network, from news sites to blogs. Think of a wedding planner showing off stunning ceremony photos in banner ads, or a home cleaning service displaying spotless kitchens on DIY websites. These visuals catch the eye and build brand awareness.

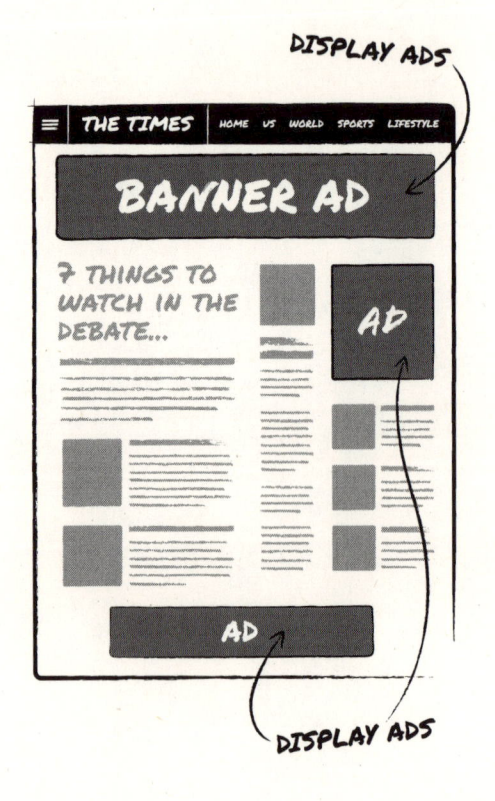

Display ads are great at reminding people about you, and this is where they really come to the fore. Imagine

ACCELERATOR 7: REACH

an online florist. Someone browses their site before Mother's Day but doesn't buy. With display ads, that florist can 'follow' the customer online for a few days, showing flower ads as they browse other sites. It's a gentle nudge saying, 'Remember us? Mum would love those flowers!'

This strategy, called retargeting, keeps your brand fresh in people's minds. It's about being seen by the right people, at the right time, in the right places.

Shopping, video, local and app

Google Shopping campaigns are similar to Facebook catalogue campaigns. They can display products from your e-commerce store directly in search results. If you are selling handmade soap, for example, shopping campaigns advertise your products in relevant Google searches, including users' preferred ingredients and scent combinations. Google Ads' non-disruptive nature is a key advantage here, as the shopping experience feels smooth and uninterrupted.

Google video campaigns primarily run through YouTube. They let you use video content to promote your product or service within relevant clips. Video campaigns can be great for capturing attention, increasing brand awareness or promoting specific products.

Local Services campaigns focus on driving foot traffic to physical retail stores, offices, restaurants, theatres, cinemas and more. They show ads across Google, including Maps, YouTube, and Search and Display networks. Closely linked to Google My

Business accounts, which play a crucial role for local businesses, local campaigns are optimised to attract people in your business's local geographical area.

App campaigns promote the download and installation of mobile apps. Google uses its algorithm to optimise the placement of your app ads in Google search, within Google Play, on YouTube or in other apps across its network.

Performance Max

Performance Max campaigns are a relatively new addition to Google Campaigns. They use Google's AI to optimise ad placements, including what you pay. This campaign type is designed to drive performance – in winning leads, for example – with minimal human input. If you are new to Google Ads, it might be sensible to choose Performance Max as your campaign type, as you don't have to do much thinking. You just tell Google about your product or service and your target market, and then let it go and do its thing.

Local Services ads

Google Guaranteed ads are part of Google's Local Services ads programme. They're designed specifically for local service businesses like plumbers, electricians, locksmiths and other home service providers. These ads are different from the standard Google Ads campaigns we talked about earlier.

Here's how they work:

- Google Guaranteed ads appear at the very top of search results, even above the regular paid ads.

- They come with a green 'Google Guaranteed' badge, which tells potential customers that Google backs the business.

- If a customer isn't happy with the work, Google might actually refund the service cost (up to a limit).

- These ads are pay-per-lead rather than pay-per-click, which means you only pay when someone actually contacts you through the ad.

To get the Google Guaranteed badge, businesses have to go through a pretty rigorous screening process. Google verifies things like licences and insurance and runs background checks. They're not available for every type of business or in every location, but for local service providers who can use them, they can be a really powerful tool. It's like getting Google's stamp of approval right there in the search results.

Retargeting ads: Turning lost opportunities into sales

Ever noticed how that electrician you looked up seems to be following you around the internet? That's retargeting in action, and it's a brilliant tool for service businesses like yours.

LEADS MACHINE

PROSPECT → YOUR SITE → PROSPECT IS TRACKED → PROSPECT LEAVES → YOUR AD ON OTHER SITES

Here's how it works: a potential client visits your website, maybe checks out your services or even starts to book an appointment, but then... they're gone. Without retargeting, you might never see or find them again. But with it? You get another shot at winning their business.

Retargeting is like a digital reminder. It follows your website visitors around the web, showing them ads based on the services they were looking at. It's why that accountant you were considering keeps popping up when you're just trying to read the news.

Why is it so effective for service businesses? Well, these aren't random people you're (re)targeting – they've already shown interest in what you offer. They just need a gentle reminder. And the numbers are impressive:

- People who see retargeted ads are 70% more likely to buy than new visitors[26]
- These ads get clicked ten times more often than regular ones

---

[26] A Hallur, '40+ retargeting statistics that are hard to ignore' (Blogging X, 23 September 2020), https://bloggingx.com/retargeting-statistics, accessed October 2024

ACCELERATOR 7: REACH

- Use retargeting with other ad techniques, and you could see 147% more bookings[27]

Let's say you're a personal trainer. Someone checks out your fitness packages but doesn't book. With retargeting, you can keep reminding them about your special intro offer or success stories. When they finally decide to get fit, guess who they'll think of?

To make the most of retargeting for your service business, there are a few key strategies to keep in mind. First off, it's crucial to segment your audience. You wouldn't talk to a potential client interested in your premium offerings the same way you'd chat with someone who's just had a quick look at your homepage, right? Tailor your ads accordingly.

Next, remember that less is often more. While you want to stay on people's radar, bombarding them with ads every five minutes is likely to put them off rather than draw them in. Strike a balance – be present, but not pushy.

Your ads need to grab attention, too. A snappy headline can work wonders, and offering something like a free consultation can be just the nudge someone needs to get back in touch. Put yourself in your clients' shoes and think about what would make you click.

Don't forget we're living in a mobile-first world. These days, many people are searching for services

---

[27] Xigen, 'What is retargeting?' (12 June 2024), https://xigen.co.uk/insights/what-is-retargeting, accessed 13 November 2024

on their phones, so make sure your ads look good on smaller screens. There's nothing worse than a jumbled, hard-to-read ad when you're trying to find a locksmith in a hurry!

Lastly, don't be afraid to experiment. What works for one service business might not work for another. Try out different ad designs, play around with your copy and test various landing pages. Keep an eye on what gets the most bookings and refine your approach over time.

Retargeting can be particularly powerful for service businesses. An emergency plumber could remind people about their twenty-four-seven call-out service. A wedding photographer could showcase their portfolio to couples who've shown interest. A lawn care service could offer seasonal discounts to previous website visitors.

Remember, retargeting is just one part of your marketing strategy. It works best alongside your other efforts. But when you get it right, it can turn those 'maybe later' clients into 'let's book now' clients. So as you're working on your Reach360 strategy, don't forget to give yourself a second chance at converting leads. With retargeting, you're not just reaching new potential clients – you're making the most of everyone who's already shown an interest in your services. It's like getting a free consultation with a warm lead – why wouldn't you take it?

The nine commandments of digital advertising success

Regardless of which type of campaign or advertising platform you choose, there are some fundamental rules that will help you reach a wider audience and scale your business in a consistent, predictable manner. These nine principles provide a framework for creating and managing successful digital advertising campaigns:

1. **Aim with precision:** Get clear on your campaign goals

2. **Know thy audience:** Understand your market and tailor your ads

3. **Budget like a boss:** Establish and adjust your advertising budget

4. **Spy with strategy:** Master keyword and competitor research

5. **Create killer ad creative:** Don't be boring

6. **Perfect the landing:** Optimise your landing page for maximum conversions

7. **Play by the rules:** Stay compliant with advertising regulations

8. **Track like a pro:** Set up your tracking and analytics correctly

9. **Decode the data:** Analyse insights and refine your approach

1. Aim with precision: Get clear on your campaign goals

The first thing you need to do is get clear on your goal. As a service business, it's crucial to know exactly what you want to achieve with your campaign. Are you trying to get more people to visit your website, generate leads, boost your brand's visibility or fill up your appointment book? Whatever it is, your goal will guide the type of campaign you run and how you measure its success. Without a clear objective, it's tough to tell if your efforts are actually paying off and if your business is growing the way you want.

As well as having a specific campaign objective, your campaigns need to be pursuing an overall goal. For service businesses, having a clear goal is everything. Unlike selling products, where you can easily track units sold, service businesses focus on attracting leads, booking appointments, getting new clients and keeping them around (retention). Whether you want to become the go-to expert in your field, bring in more clients or keep your existing ones coming back, knowing what you're aiming for helps you stay on track and ensures your campaigns deliver results.

This is especially true for paid advertising campaigns. With a well-defined objective, your ads – whether on Google, Facebook or any other platform – will target the right audience, use the best ad formats and give you a solid ROI. That way, your ads aren't just reaching more people, they're reaching the *right* people, making all the difference in driving your service business forward.

2. Know thy audience: Understand your market and tailor your ads

The second principle is to use all the insights you have gained through studying and understanding your market. You should know who your customers are (they're not 'everyone'), what they need and how they search for and purchase solutions. You need to know what their pain points are and possible objections to buying. You will also want to use demographic, geographic and preference data: are they of a certain age? Are you predominantly selling products to men or women? Where are your customers based, geographically? What hobbies and interests do they have? You can use all the data captured from surveys and engagement metrics to build a detailed profile of your target audience, as discussed in earlier chapters. To scale up your business and drive it forward, we will use all this information to tailor your ads and choose targeting options that will best reach new potential customers.

3. Budget like a boss: Establish and adjust your advertising budget

Starting out with a clear budget in mind is key for any advertising campaign, but if you're just getting started with paid ads, establishing the right amount isn't always straightforward. Spend too much too quickly and you may end up burning through your advertising budget and not having enough left to acquire data over time and optimise your campaign. Spend too little, and you won't have a big enough sample size to be able to make data-driven decisions.

When I discuss advertising budgets with service businesses, many are uncertain and seek my advice. The reality is there's no universal answer to how much you need to spend. But if you've been applying the lessons of this book, you should have a good grasp of your average cost per lead. This figure is crucial as it allows you to work backwards and establish a target advertising budget to generate your desired number of leads.

Let's consider an example. Say you're running a solar installation business with a cost per lead of $100 and your goal is to generate twenty leads per month. In this case, your initial monthly budget would be around $2,000 a month. However, it's important to note that your target budget isn't static. It can fluctuate based on various factors such as seasonality, cultural events and geographical considerations, all of which can influence the cost of your advertising. The advertising budget (and CPA) of similar businesses based in New York City (which has marked seasons) and Las Vegas (where it's mostly sunny all year round) will be different, for example.

By starting with this baseline budget and remaining flexible, you can adjust your spending as you gather more data and insights. This approach allows you to optimise your advertising spend over time, ensuring you're getting the best return on your investment while meeting your lead generation goals.

The thing about digital advertising is that it's all about gathering data, testing what works and then fine-tuning your approach. This means your budget needs to be somewhat flexible, ready to change as your campaigns develop. I like to call it a 'testing budget'. You might start with some budget predictions based on educated guesses, but you won't know the real numbers until you're up and running. So if you don't have a budget that you're prepared to potentially lose in the short term – to enable data collection and campaign optimisation for long-term ROI – you might not be ready for paid ads just yet. This initial investment is crucial for learning and fine-tuning your approach.

4. Spy with strategy: Master keyword and competitor research

The fourth principle is keyword research. If you're running search campaigns, you absolutely need to understand how your potential customers are searching online.

Fortunately, Google makes it easy with its free Keyword Planner tool, conveniently built right into the Ads platform. This tool helps you find the search terms that are most relevant to your products or services, making it a crucial resource for any campaign. As mentioned earlier, with AI rapidly advancing, tools like Performance Max campaigns mean Google's AI can handle much of the keyword research and optimisation for you. This is a great option if you prefer a more hands-off approach.

However, if you want more specific control and truly understand the nuances of your market, mastering the art of identifying and targeting the best keywords in your campaigns will be incredibly valuable. Knowing exactly which keywords to target can make all the difference in your campaign's success.

You've already scoped out your competition, and it's important that you track what strategies they're using. The Facebook Ads Library offers great insights into their ads, but don't overlook what they're doing on Google. Identifying the keywords they're targeting and the search terms they're ranking for is crucial.

Tools like SEMRush, Ahrefs, SpyFu and AdLab can help you uncover which keywords your competitors are bidding on and how they're performing in search results. By analysing these strategies, you can refine your own keyword targeting and ensure you're not missing out on key opportunities.

PRO TIP

For a service-based business, like a plumbing company, you can use Google Keyword Planner to discover high-intent keywords that your potential customers are searching for, like 'emergency plumber near me' or '24-hour plumbing service'.

Here's how you do it: put these phrases into the Keyword Planner, and it'll show you related keywords

> along with their search volumes and competition levels. Let's say you find that 'emergency plumbing repair' has a high search volume but low competition in your area – that's a keyword you'll want to target in your campaigns. By focusing on these specific, high-intent keywords, you can attract customers who are ready to book your services right now.

5. Create killer ad creative: Don't be boring

The fifth principle is to craft compelling copy and design strong creative elements. Your ads need to be engaging, relevant and crystal clear in their call to action. It's not enough to just grab attention; your ads should guide viewers on exactly what to do next. Whether it's clicking a link, signing up or making a purchase, the path forward should be obvious.

Example 1: Martial arts academy
What everyone else does:

- **Copy:** 'Join our martial arts academy.'
- **Design:** A generic image of a martial arts class with no clear focus.
- **CTA:** A small, vague button that just says 'Learn more.'

This ad lacks urgency, relevance and a clear directive. The message is too broad, the image doesn't stand out and the call to action doesn't give a compelling reason to click. It's easy for potential customers to scroll past this ad without a second thought.

How to stand out:

- **Copy:** 'Boost your child's confidence with martial arts – get your first class free!'
- **Design:** A high-quality image of a child in a martial arts uniform, smiling and looking confident, with bold text highlighting the free class offer.
- **CTA:** A large, eye-catching button that says 'Claim your free class!'

This ad is targeted, appealing and action oriented. It speaks directly to parents looking to help their child gain confidence, offers a tangible benefit (a free class) and makes it easy for them to take the next step. The visuals reinforce the message by showcasing a positive outcome.

Example 2: Landscaping company

What everyone else does:

- **Copy:** 'Landscaping and gardening services.'
- **Design:** A basic image of a lawn with no distinct features.
- **CTA:** A small button that says 'Contact us.'

This ad is too generic and doesn't highlight any specific benefits or services. The image is bland and the call to action is weak and uninspiring. It doesn't give the viewer any real incentive to click or learn more.

How to stand out:

- **Copy:** 'Transform your backyard – get 20% off your first landscaping project!'

- **Design:** A vibrant image of a beautifully landscaped backyard with a before-and-after contrast, showcasing a dramatic improvement.

- **CTA:** A prominent button that says 'Get your free quote!'

See what I'm getting at? When your ads are specific, visually appealing and have a strong call to action, they're way more likely to grab attention and actually get results. It's all about showing people exactly what you can do for them and making it super easy for them to take the next step. So whether you're running a martial arts academy or a landscaping business, focus on clear benefits, eye-catching visuals and a CTA that makes people want to click. Trust me, it makes all the difference.

6. Perfect the landing: Optimise your landing page for maximum conversions

Commandment six is all about optimising your landing page to drive up conversions. We've already talked about how crucial landing pages are but seriously, the last thing you want is to send people to a page that's incoherent or worse, non-functional. Imagine clicking on an ad only for the page to take ages to load, the text being impossible to read, the video not playing, or the button not working. It's incredibly frustrating.

It always amazes me how many service businesses run Google Ads and just send people straight to their website – a website that's often poorly designed, crammed with a mishmash of services and topped off with a generic contact form. In today's competitive landscape, that simply won't cut it.

What you need is a landing page that's laser focused on converting visitors. That means clear CTAs, a prominently displayed phone number, ideally a real-time webchat powered by an AI bot and tracking of phone numbers to monitor your leads. And don't forget a strong incentive to capture data, like a lead magnet that encourages visitors to take the next step.

7. Play by the rules: Stay compliant with advertising regulations

The seventh commandment is to play by the rules – this is especially important if you're in a highly regulated field like healthcare or finance. If you want to advertise on platforms like Facebook, Google, LinkedIn or TikTok, you need to play by their rules. Closely. This isn't a free-for-all; break the rules and you risk getting your ad account restricted – or even worse, banned forever. Imagine not being able to advertise again, or losing years of precious data and having to start again from scratch. It's just not worth it.

ACCELERATOR 7: REACH

Most digital advertising platforms have strict policies against misleading or offensive content, and there are special restrictions for ads in areas like housing, employment and credit products. Health-related ads and products like alcohol also have extra rules. There are too many specific policies to list here (and honestly, some can be quite ambiguous or vague) but a quick Google search (eg, 'Google advertising policies') will give you the details.

The bottom line? Either stay on top of the latest rules, or work with agencies and partners who are on the ball. That way, your ads will not only reach more people but you'll also keep your account safe and your campaigns running smoothly.

8. Track like a pro: Set up your tracking and analytics correctly

This principle is all about making sure your tracking and analytics are properly configured. Use the right tracking pixels, conversion events and tools like Facebook's API to gather accurate data on how users interact with your ads, who visits your website and which clicks convert into sales. Getting this set up correctly is essential to understanding your campaign's performance.

9. Decode the data: Analyse insights and refine your approach

Once your tracking is in place, the next step is to dive into the data. Pay attention to the insights you're getting and be ready to adjust your strategy based on what it's telling you. The trick is to never stop testing – experiment with different ad formats, creative ideas and targeting options to find out what resonates most. Even experienced digital advertisers can be surprised by the data, so it's important to stay flexible. Remember, not every campaign will be a winner, but there's no such thing as failure – just learning that gets you closer to success. This cycle of constant refinement is crucial for long-term success.

These, my friends, are the mechanisms, strategies and commandments for reaching more people and putting your business in front of more people than you could ever dream of with paid online advertising. Isn't it amazing? It's a great time to run a small business or be an entrepreneur. With these advertising platforms a world of clients and customers are at your fingertips.

Now that your system is set up to reach a wider audience, we can move on to the next Drive accelerator: Resell. There we're talking about how to keep all those new customers we've reached for as long as possible, increasing purchase frequency and remarketing to maximise every penny of your marketing spend.

Let's do it.

> **For exclusive *Leads Machine* tools and resources visit: https://francisrodino.com/tools**

11

Accelerator 8: Resell – Turn Customers Into Raving Fans And Repeat Buyers

In the last chapter, we talked about how to reach new customers with paid ads. In this chapter, I'm going to cover our 'Resell' accelerator. This is all about turning those one-time buyers into loyal, repeat customers. After all, why settle for a single sale when you can create a steady stream of repeat business?

Cast your mind back to our Revenue Growth Formula. Remember how increasing purchase frequency is one of the key dials you can adjust to boost your sales and revenue? Well, that's exactly what we're doing here. It's about maximising the value of each customer relationship you've worked so hard to establish. It will always be cheaper to sell to customers who know you than to attract new buyers.

So here's my question:

LEADS MACHINE

How effectively are you maximising revenue from each customer through repeat purchases, upselling and re-engaging past customers?

1	2	3	4	5	6	7	8	9	10
No Idea 'We currently do not re-engage past customers, missing significant opportunities for additional revenue.'			**Sparking Interest** 'We occasionally reach out to past customers, but there is no consistent strategy in place.'				**Leading Sales Growth** 'We operate a slick, automated system that reactivates past customers and drives new sales efficiently.'		

If you're already excelling at reselling to your existing customers, congratulations! You're ahead of the game. But for those of you who feel there's room for improvement, don't worry – I've got you covered. In this chapter, I'll be sharing some powerful strategies to boost your reselling efforts.

At the heart of these strategies is your CRM system. By tapping into the data in your CRM, and listening to insights about your customer interactions, their preferences and purchase history, you can create marketing campaigns that feel personal and relevant to each customer.

You can use the knowledge you've built up of where people click, how they browse and respond to your ads, and data around interest and preferences to present new and irresistible offers. You can also use loyalty programmes to reward repeat purchases, encourage people to buy more frequently and tempt them back to you for continued services or more products.

There are fully automated email campaigns to consider too. These can work tirelessly in the background, re-engaging customers with personalised recommendations and timely updates. It's like having a super-efficient sales team working round the clock.

Selling more to existing customers

Struggling to find ideas on what you can resell? Trust me, there are more opportunities than you might think. Take personal trainers, for instance. They're not just about one-off sessions. Smart trainers are upselling monthly packages, throwing in nutritional planning and even offering online support between gym visits. It's all about maximising that client relationship.

Hair salons are another great example. They're not just cutting and colouring – they're selling professional hair care products, loyalty programmes for regular treatments and even styling lessons. Every client who walks out the door is a potential repeat customer.

IT support companies? They're transitioning from reactive fix-it jobs to proactive maintenance contracts. They're adding cybersecurity packages and hardware upgrades to their offerings. It's about being the go-to tech partner, not just the emergency call-out.

Even accountants are getting in on the act. They're not just doing the books anymore – they're offering tax planning, payroll services and annual financial health checks. They're positioning themselves as a financial partner, not just a number-cruncher.

Wedding photographers are thinking beyond the big day. They're selling album design services, promoting family photoshoots to newlyweds and offering canvas prints. They're turning a one-time gig into a lifelong relationship.

Plumbers are installing boilers and then selling annual service contracts. They're promoting water softeners and bathroom renovations. Every call-out is a chance to upsell.

Dentists are brightening smiles with whitening services, promoting cosmetic options and selling electric toothbrushes. They're not just fixing teeth – they're selling the whole package of oral health.

Digital marketing agencies are constantly evolving their offerings. SEO, social media management, website redesigns – they're always finding new ways to add value for their clients.

Even lawn care services are getting creative. They're offering seasonal services, promoting landscaping design and selling lawn care products. They're not just mowing lawns – they're creating outdoor lifestyles.

And car mechanics? They're selling annual service packages, promoting tyre services and even offering car detailing. They're aiming to be your car's best friend for life.

The common thread here? These businesses are all thinking beyond the initial sale. They're looking at their customers' ongoing needs and finding ways to meet them. They're building relationships, not just chasing transactions. It's not about being pushy – it's about being helpful, anticipating needs and offering solutions.

Remember, every interaction with a customer is a chance to add value and potentially make another sale. And with your CRM and marketing automation, you can set this up so it all happens without you.

So take a look at your business model. What additional services or products could you offer? How can you turn a one-time customer into a lifelong client? The possibilities are endless – you just need to start thinking creatively, and try to create a 'value ladder' that repeat clients and customers can climb up.

Maximising ROI with a value ladder

When investing in digital advertising, your goal is to maximise return on investment (ROI). However, true profitability often comes from nurturing clients through a well-designed value ladder, not just from the initial offer.

Consider a digital marketing agency; their value ladder might look something like this:

1. Free SEO audit (lead magnet)

2. $500 website optimisation (entry-level service)

3. $2,000/month full-service digital marketing package

4. $10,000 complete digital transformation consultation

This value ladder allows the agency to attract leads with a free, valuable offer, convert them with an affordable entry-level service and then resell them more comprehensive, higher-value services.

Let's break it down:

Say your cost per lead is $100. You generate ten leads for $1,000. Two leads buy the website optimisation service, bringing in $1,000. You've broken even, but the real value is yet to come. One of these clients later upgrades to the monthly package. Over a year, that's $24,000. The other opts for the digital transformation consultation. You've now turned your $1,000 ad spend into $35,000 in revenue.

This demonstrates the power of reselling to existing clients. These clients already know and trust you, making them more receptive to higher-value offerings. Some businesses balk at customer acquisition costs, but it's the path to growth. Whether it's through digital marketing, networking or traditional advertising, acquiring customers is an investment, not just an expense. By focusing on a client's lifetime value rather than just the initial sale, your marketing spend becomes an investment in long-term relationships. Your ROI isn't about a single transaction – it's about building trust over time, leading to ongoing business and valuable referrals.

Successful reselling means viewing your marketing efforts and investment as the beginning of a journey with your clients, not just a one-off transaction. This approach turns your marketing spend into a powerful engine for sustainable business growth.

There are many businesses out there who build trust well, but the obvious example is Apple. They've achieved tremendous growth and maintained an extremely loyal customer base. Fans are 'Apple for life' and excitedly celebrate each new product release like it is Christmas. There is no fear of buying from Apple because they offer quality and perceived value. They've built their brand reputation so well that customers actively look forward to spending their cash with them. 'Here, take my money!'

It is clear that Apple invests heavily in customer retention. Once people buy a product, they enter a carefully engineered ecosystem. All Apple devices work seamlessly together. If I have an Apple Watch and an iMac, why would I buy another brand of smartphone? I know an iPhone is going to slot right in. Apple maximises its customer lifetime value by releasing an iPhone every year and new Mac laptop models regularly, continually delivering performance upgrades and creating subscription services like Apple Music, iCloud and Apple TV. All of these things ensure customers spend money with them rather than their competitors and stay with them over time. Apple's branding is everywhere. You don't necessarily see their reselling strategies, but this is how they have made trillions of dollars – building loyalty and trust.

When I think about trust, another mammoth brand that springs to mind is Amazon. It has absolutely crushed its competition through convenience. If you have a problem with anything you've bought, they will sort you out, no questions asked. Even if a product breaks further down the line, they'll help you out, send you a new one or refund you because they understand that trust wins out in the long run. Amazon are also experts when it comes to bundling products – we've all experienced their convincing recommendations at checkout.

Another giant, Nike, utilises its Nike Membership, Nike Training Club, Nike Run Club and more to foster strong relationships with its customers. They use these digital services to collect customer preferences, send personalised offers, cross-sell aligned products, give customers access to new products and provide exclusive content. This all drives repeat purchases and increases their ROI. Nike definitely recognises that retaining customers costs less than acquiring new ones.

While it's easy to think that the loyalty-building strategies of giants like Apple, Amazon and Nike are out of reach for smaller service businesses, the core principles behind their success are universal. As a service business owner, you can adapt these strategies to fit your scale and niche. Create your own ecosystem of complementary services, focus relentlessly on customer experience and leverage digital tools to engage and retain clients. Use your CRM system to personalise offerings, foster a sense of community among your customers and consistently innovate to keep them engaged.

The goal isn't to replicate these titans exactly, but to understand and creatively apply the principles behind their success. Whether you're a solo consultant or running a small team, you can build stronger, more profitable relationships with your customers by focusing on creating value, building trust and continuous engagement. By doing so, you'll create your own loyal fan base – customers who eagerly anticipate your services and become your best advocates. Remember, at its core, this is about creating an experience so good that your customers can't wait to see what you'll offer next, regardless of the size of your business.

Loyalty pays: Building a base of repeat customers

Loyalty programmes are a powerful tool for encouraging repeat business, and they're not just for big chains. From Starbucks' sophisticated app-based system to the humble punch card at your local café, these programmes all serve the same purpose: rewarding customer loyalty and incentivising repeat purchases.

They're not just for coffee shops and airlines anymore. Even your local electrician or accountant can get in on this game. For service businesses, you could put in place a points system where clients earn credit towards future services, or a tiered programme where your regulars unlock premium perks. The key is to keep it simple and offer rewards that your clients will actually use.

Think about what would make your clients say, 'Yep, I'm sticking with this business.' For example, an IT support company could offer priority service after a certain number of contracts. A premium landscaping service might regularly offer special discounts or priority scheduling to their long-term clients. A personal trainer might throw in a free nutrition consultation when clients book a package of sessions. The possibilities are endless – just make sure it fits your business model and what your clients value.

Offering exclusive deals and promotions for existing customers is a super effective strategy to build loyalty and trust. The sense of belonging to an exclusive group with unique perks resonates with customers and since, as we know, the cost of retaining customers is lower than acquiring new ones, providing discounts to this select group has less impact on overall margins, which can significantly boost your RO and turn customer loyalty into profit.

There are plenty of other strategies you can use to fuel your Resell strategy, which we'll discuss in the following sections.

Personalisation: Making your clients feel like VIPs

Personalisation (personalised marketing) uses your customer data to create tailored messages and recommendations, encouraging repeat business

ACCELERATOR 8: RESELL

and fostering loyalty. You don't need Amazon-level resources to achieve this; even small service businesses can implement effective personalisation strategies. Consider these examples:

- A physiotherapist sends exercise videos tailored to a client's specific injury
- An auto mechanic reminds customers of upcoming services based on their vehicle's mileage
- A dog groomer offers breed-specific grooming tips and product recommendations
- A language tutor suggests learning materials based on a student's proficiency level and interests
- An interior designer shares personalised mood boards inspired by a client's previous choices

These approaches show customers that you understand their unique needs. By leveraging existing data, you create meaningful interactions that drive engagement and repeat business. Remember, effective personalisation is about using the information you have available (stored in your CRM system) to make each customer feel valued and understood.

Building recurring revenue through subscriptions

While it's easy to think that subscriptions are only for streaming services or product deliveries, the subscription model is increasingly relevant across various service sectors.

Just a few examples:

- A personal trainer offers monthly coaching packages with customised workout plans
- An IT support company provides ongoing tech assistance for a fixed monthly fee
- A lawn care service delivers regular maintenance and seasonal treatments
- A business consultant offers weekly strategy sessions and resource access
- A car detailing service sells a monthly package for regular upkeep

There are so many advantages to the subscription model. Clients receive a consistent, reliable service, for a fixed monthly fee, while businesses enjoy a steady revenue stream. It's an approach that can help smooth out the financial peaks and troughs many service businesses experience. Subscriptions also foster ongoing client relationships, increasing engagement and loyalty. This provides opportunities for upselling and cross-selling as you become more familiar with your clients' needs over time.

Think about what aspects of your service could be packaged into a recurring offering. You can get creative here. Even if it's not initially obvious, there may be more potential in your business model than you realise. Putting in place a subscription service can lead to more predictable income and stronger client relationships.

Cross-selling, upselling and bundling

Remember, if you're not making offers, prospects and clients don't have the opportunity to buy from you. Cross-selling, upselling and bundling are great ways for you to put more offers in front of your clients and so maximise each client interaction.

Cross-selling involves offering complementary services alongside the main service a client is buying, and upselling encourages clients to opt for a higher-tier or more comprehensive version of the service they're considering.

But huge opportunities lie in combining multiple services into a package deal, a 'bundle', often at a slight discount compared to buying each service separately. The great thing about bundles is that they can be your 'unique mechanism' (see the Magnetic Messaging chapter).

Here are some examples of how you can apply these techniques:

- Web design and digital services:
    - Cross-selling: Offering hosting and maintenance packages alongside website creation
    - Upselling: Encouraging clients to upgrade from a basic website to a premium e-commerce platform
    - Bundle: 'Digital Presence Boost' package including website design, twelve months of hosting and three months of SEO services
- Accounting and financial services:
    - Cross-selling: Proposing tax planning services when preparing annual returns
    - Upselling: Suggesting a more comprehensive financial health check instead of basic bookkeeping
    - Bundle: 'Small Business Financial Package' including monthly bookkeeping, tax return preparation and quarterly financial advice sessions
- Personal training and wellness:
    - Cross-selling: Offering nutritional counselling to complement workout plans

- Upselling: Encouraging clients to upgrade from group classes to personalised one-on-one training

- Bundle: 'Total Transformation Package' including weekly training sessions, customised meal plans, and monthly progress assessments

- Hair and beauty services:

    - Cross-selling: Recommending professional hair care products after a cut and colour

    - Upselling: Suggesting a premium treatment (eg, keratin treatment) in addition to a regular haircut

    - Bundle: 'Complete Makeover Package' including haircut, colour, facial and a set of salon-quality hair care products

The key, as always, is to ensure that your additional offerings provide genuine value. It's not about pushing unnecessary services, but about identifying and fulfilling additional needs your clients may have. Remember, the purpose of selling is to serve, and cross-selling and upselling can enhance the client experience while boosting your revenue. Think creatively about how you can apply these techniques in your business to provide more comprehensive solutions for your clients.

Beyond the sale: Turning clients into raving fans

The sale is just the beginning. What happens after a customer makes a purchase plays a huge role in how they perceive your brand. Staying in touch after the sale keeps them engaged and makes it more likely they'll return. Not only does this boost repeat purchases, but it also encourages referrals, testimonials and helps build a stellar reputation. Simple actions like follow-up emails with care tips for their purchase, asking for feedback, or sharing relevant content can make a big difference.

Companies like Apple, Amazon, and Nike have mastered this, but it's something any business can do. Take a high-end spa, for example – they might send a personalised thank you note after each visit, followed by emails with skincare tips or wellness advice. These are classy tips that don't go unnoticed. They could even send a reminder when it's time for your next appointment based on your past treatments. For a busy professional, that little nudge to book your next rejuvenation session can turn an ordinary visit into a much-anticipated treat.

The 'wow' factor

Creating a 'wow' factor in your customer service is another powerful way to build trust, encourage loyalty and drive repeat business. While many companies talk about prioritising customer satisfaction, they often stumble when asked about specific tools or systems for delivering exceptional experiences.

Let's take one of our clients, Help Me Fix, as an example. They're revolutionising the trades industry by bringing remote diagnosis to homeowners, connecting them with contractors to diagnose and fix minor issues in their homes. It's essentially like Uber for home repairs.

One of their standout features is a new AI tool, similar to ChatGPT, that allows homeowners to find solutions, advice, resources and tips for all their home problems at their fingertips, instantly. This AI-powered assistant is available twenty-four-seven, providing immediate responses to queries that might otherwise require waiting for a tradesperson to be available. Imagine a homeowner discovering a leaky tap at 2am. Instead of panicking or waiting until morning to call a plumber, they can immediately consult the AI tool. It might guide them through a simple fix they can do themselves, or help them understand the severity of the problem, advising whether it's safe to wait or if emergency services are needed.

This level of instant, personalised support creates a genuine 'wow' moment. It's not just solving problems; it's empowering homeowners with knowledge and confidence. The AI can also learn from each interaction, becoming smarter and more helpful over time. It might start recognising patterns in the issues occurring in a particular home, suggesting preventative maintenance to avoid future problems.

The exciting thing about this technology is that it's transforming an industry traditionally reliant on in-person services. Help Me Fix is setting a new standard for customer service in the trades sector (their 'unique mechanism'), blending the irreplaceable skills of human tradespeople with the instant, always-on support of AI.

This approach doesn't just solve immediate problems – it builds a relationship with customers. Homeowners are likely to return to a service that's always there for them, ready with helpful advice or quick connections to qualified professionals when needed. It's a perfect example of how technology can be used to create that 'wow' factor, driving customer loyalty and encouraging repeat business.

Customer feedback – your growth engine

Harnessing customer feedback is a powerful strategy for building trust and driving sales. It's not only about collecting nice reviews – it's about starting real conversations and collecting data that you can use to transform your business.

Let's take the example of a local physiotherapy clinic putting this into action. They set up a simple online feedback system where clients can rate their sessions. Using this information, they create a 'Treatment of the Month' – a technique that gets rave reviews from patients. It's a great way to build a relationship, provide a 'wow' service and get people coming back.

ACCELERATOR 8: RESELL

But here's where it gets really interesting. The clinic could use a tool like ScoreApp to create a smart questionnaire for patients. It's like a mini check-up where patients input their symptoms and lifestyle factors, and out pops a personalised treatment suggestion. Picture this: a patient with nagging back pain fills out the scorecard. Based on their answers, the app recommends a mix of specific exercises, hands-on techniques and maybe some lifestyle tweaks. It's healthcare tailored just for them and best of all, it's fully automated. You are providing value, twenty-four-seven.

This approach is brilliant on multiple levels. It gets patients involved in their own care, gives the clinic loads of useful data and makes each patient feel like they're getting a bespoke, personalised service. When clients feel like they're being heard, they're more likely to stick around and tell their friends about the great service they've had. From their side, the clinic can use all this information to shape and improve their services. They might spot trends and create new programmes that really hit the mark for their patients. It's a win-win situation that can really drive your business forward.

So don't just collect feedback – use it to power up your business. Your clients' insights could be the key to setting yourself apart from the competition and fuelling your growth. It's not rocket science, but it is pretty powerful stuff.

CRM: The beating heart of your reselling strategy

As we've learned through this chapter, reselling to existing customers is far easier than selling to new ones. The great thing about all of these powerful resell strategies is that they can all be automated through a modern CRM system. Lots of people ask me, 'Which CRM should I use?' The answer is 'the one that you use'. A CRM system on its own is an empty shell. You'll need a great strategy and system if you're looking to scale up with online ads. If you're not actively using it to engage, communicate and sell, even the most sophisticated system becomes nothing more than an expensive address book.

Setting up and optimising a CRM can be a daunting task, especially when you're already juggling the day-to-day demands of running a business, but the lessons in this book should help. Remember, the goal isn't just to have a CRM – it's to have a CRM that works for you, driving engagement, streamlining communication and boosting sales. Whether you decide to go it alone or seek expert help, the important thing is to take that first step towards leveraging the power of a well-implemented CRM system.

The road ahead

Congratulations! You've now got some battle-tested systems and strategies to understand your market, craft compelling offers and messages and create a

ACCELERATOR 8: RESELL

well-thought-out customer journey. You should also have a thorough understanding of paid advertising channels, along with strategies and tactics to sell and resell to both new and existing customers. You've got a solid foundation in place: a compelling landing page, an irresistible lead magnet, enticing offers and a robust CRM system to capture and nurture leads until they convert. You've also developed a strategy for customer retention and reselling. It's tempting to think your work is done, but in the world of automated digital marketing, there's no such thing as 'set and forget'. This is all fantastic groundwork, but it's really just the beginning. A long road of evolving and refining your marketing system lies ahead.

Think of your marketing system as a living, breathing entity. It needs constant attention and refinement to thrive. Once real performance data starts flowing in, you'll need to be ready to respond and adapt. Your initial setup is your best educated guess, but the real magic happens when you start fine-tuning based on actual results.

Are your ads hitting the mark? Is your landing page converting as well as you'd hoped? Are your email sequences engaging customers or falling flat? These are the questions you'll need to answer as you move forward.

Remember, the digital landscape is always evolving, and so should your marketing strategies. Stay tuned as we explore how to keep your newly scaled business model not just running, but constantly improving and adapting to the changing market dynamics.

> For exclusive *Leads Machine* tools and resources visit: https://francisrodino.com/tools

12
Accelerator 9: Refine – Optimise Your Marketing For Lasting Success

In our final accelerator, Refine, we turn our focus to tuning the engine that drives your business forward. Imagine it as routine maintenance for your marketing machine – it's not about overhauling the whole system, but making those precise, data-driven adjustments that keep it running at peak performance. I'll introduce you to the Optimisation Oracle, my method for continually fine-tuning and enhancing your marketing efforts. By learning to interpret performance metrics and using data to guide each tweak, you'll ensure your business remains agile and efficient. This ongoing process of testing, learning and optimising will keep your business in the fast lane, ready to tackle whatever the road ahead holds. The Optimisation Oracle involves analysing your key metrics – clicks, conversions, costs and profits – to gauge the effectiveness of your campaigns. It's rare to hit the sweet spot on your first attempt, so be prepared to iterate.

The digital marketing process is all about experimentation. This might involve refreshing your ad creatives, testing different headlines, crafting new CTAs or selecting alternative images. Sometimes, it's not about changing the ad itself but reallocating your budget. If Google isn't delivering quality leads, you might shift that spend to Facebook where you're seeing better results. Don't forget to experiment with your landing pages and tweak your offers too.

Read the question below – where do you think you score?

How effectively are you measuring and optimising each touchpoint in your marketing system to ensure you are consistently maximising ROI?

1	2	3	4	5	6	7	8	9	10
Flying Blind 'We currently do not measure the performance of our marketing touchpoints, missing critical insights into ROI.'			**Emerging Optimisation** 'We monitor some key marketing touchpoints but lack a comprehensive system to measure everything effectively.'				**Optimisation Mastery** 'We have a comprehensive system in place that measures and optimises every marketing touchpoint for maximum ROI.'		

The reality is that measurement and refinement of your marketing system never stops. It's a bit like

ACCELERATOR 9: REFINE

being a scientist, methodically testing hypotheses to uncover breakthrough insights. Every test, every tweak, every moment of inspired curiosity is a step towards marketing excellence.

The Refine accelerator embodies this philosophy. It's not about dramatic overhauls, but rather implementing a series of small, data-driven tweaks. These incremental improvements, when compounded over time, can lead to significant enhancements in your marketing performance. By embracing this mindset of continuous optimisation, you ensure your automated marketing machine stays finely tuned and ahead of the curve in an ever-evolving digital landscape.

As I mentioned earlier, data is the new gold. Savvy service providers understand this. As a business owner, it's crucial to set aside gut feelings and embrace the insights that data provides about your clients and marketing efforts. Successful service companies that thrive online are continuously collecting and analysing data. A thriving physiotherapy clinic, for example, might study patient booking patterns, test different service-focused ads and fine-tune personalised follow-ups to boost repeat appointments.

Fortunately, when running digital ads, the platforms collect data for you. Google, Facebook and other major players have built-in analytics that clearly show what's working and what's not. The reality is that initially, your ads might miss the mark – that's normal. These platforms want your ads to succeed, so they've made it straightforward to spot trends, run tests and identify areas for improvement.

If you hear another service provider claim that digital marketing 'doesn't work', they've likely skipped the crucial steps of analysis, strategic thinking and creative refinement. Marketing is an iterative process. Even the most experienced marketers rarely hit a home run on their first swing. That's okay. The key is to listen to the data, make changes and keep iterating. Second, third, fourth attempts – that's often where the magic happens for service businesses.

If you've launched your ad campaign and the data reveals that the results are… well, less than stellar. What do you do next? How do you refine your approach and boost performance?

To guide you through this refinement and optimisation journey, I've created an ad optimisation cheat sheet for you. It consists of six critical questions to ask yourself that will pinpoint areas for improvement and guide your optimisation efforts.

We'll use Facebook ads as our example, but the principles apply across all major platforms, including Google. The key to refinement of any campaign lies in three key areas: ad performance, lead capture and your sales process.

Ad Optimisation Cheat Sheet

There are six questions you need to ask yourself when optimising. Work through these questions to diagnose issues and fix any 'leaks' in your ads and sales funnel, and turn your underwhelming campaign into a high-performing marketing machine.

1. Did people click on your ads?

If the answer is no, and you've got a statistically significant number of impressions (over 1,000), then low clicks suggest your ad isn't resonating with your audience. It's not grabbing their attention or compelling them to take action. Perhaps your offer isn't enticing enough, or your messaging isn't hitting the mark.

In this case, it's time to roll up your sleeves and revisit your ad creative (text and image/video). Think about your headline, imagery and copy. Are they truly speaking to your target audience's pain points and desires? Is your value proposition clear and compelling? Does your copy call out your audience and hook them in? Don't be afraid to experiment with different approaches. Sometimes, a small tweak can make a big difference in capturing your audience's interest and boosting those click-through rates.

2. Were the clicks expensive?

Remember, platforms like Facebook and Google operate on auction-based systems. You're essentially bidding against competitors to reach your target audience. If your cost per click is higher than expected, there's probably something going on.

Here's the thing about most ad platforms: they prioritise relevance. They will show less relevant ads, but at a premium. For instance, advertising Nike trainers to Adidas enthusiasts will likely be costly. The platforms want to deliver a good user experience, so they use pricing to encourage advertisers to target more appropriately. You could try selling beefburgers to vegans, but you'd pay through the nose for it.

The key is to refine your targeting. Are you reaching the right audience? Is your ad relevant to them? Improving your targeting can significantly reduce your CPC and stretch your budget further. Remember, a high CPC doesn't just eat into your budget – it's a sign that your ads might not be reaching the most receptive audience. It's worth taking the time to reassess and refine your targeting strategy.

3. Was the ad rejected or suspended?

Alas, if your ad was rejected or suspended, you're definitely not getting any clicks. All advertising platforms have strict guidelines and policies that advertisers must adhere to. If your ad has been rejected, it's likely because you've inadvertently violated these rules.

While I won't delve into the specifics here, platforms like Facebook have comprehensive policies covering everything from politics and social issues to housing, finance and health. I talked in more depth about this in the Reach accelerator chapter, and you can look up the specific policies on each platform to avoid getting your ad or your account suspended.

4. Are people clicking on the ad, but then nothing happens?

A 'bounce' is when people land on your page and then leave; Google Analytics tracks bounces for you. They can be incredibly frustrating. If users are clicking but not taking any further action, this is a red flag; it often indicates a disconnect between your ad and where it leads – be it a landing page or a lead magnet.

The journey from ad to action should be seamless. Your landing page or offer should directly relate to and expand upon what drew the user to click in the first place. If it doesn't, you risk losing potential customers at this critical juncture. Ensure there's a strong, logical link between your ad and where it leads to maximise your conversion potential.

Picture this: you're browsing online, you see an interesting ad, you click it… and suddenly you're on a page that has nothing to do with what you were looking for. Feels a bit like a bait-and-switch, doesn't it? That's when most people bounce – they leave without interacting, never to return.

It's a common pitfall, especially for tradespeople. You might see an ad for emergency plumbing, click it and end up on a general 'About us' page. Now you're forced to hunt around for the service you actually wanted. In our fast-paced world, that's a sure-fire way to lose potential customers.

Don't forget about the look and feel of your landing page. If it seems unprofessional, confusing or takes ages to load, visitors will be out faster than you can say 'conversion rate'. They'll think, 'This looks a bit dodgy,' and click away, taking their business (and your ad spend) with them.

The key is to make sure your ad and landing page are a perfect match, like fish and chips. Give people exactly what they're expecting, and make it easy for them to take the next step. That way, you'll turn those bounces into beautiful conversions.

5. Does your landing page convert?

So you've created a professional, visually appealing landing page that aligns perfectly with your ad, but people still aren't taking action. Your lead capture form sits there, empty and lonely. You're getting lots of clicks, but no opt-ins. Even if visitors don't bounce immediately, something might be holding them back.

ACCELERATOR 9: REFINE

THANK YOU PAGE

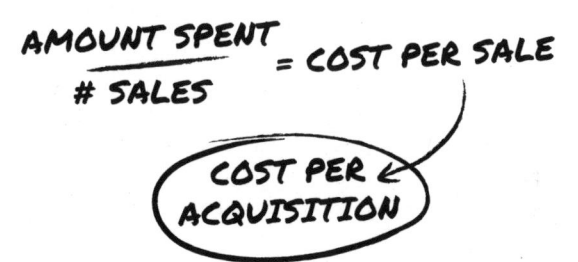

Thank you for your submission!

$$\frac{\# \text{ SALES}}{\# \text{ LEADS}} = \% \text{ SALES CLOSED}$$

$$\frac{\text{AMOUNT SPENT}}{\# \text{ SALES}} = \text{COST PER SALE}$$

(COST PER ACQUISITION)

Let's dig into what might be going wrong by working through this list:

1. First off, how's your page loading? If it's taking ages, people might be giving up before they even see your offer.

2. Next, have a look at your CTA. Is it standing out like a sore thumb (in a good way)? It should be impossible to miss.

3. Now, about your message – is it crystal clear, or might it be leaving people scratching their heads?

4. And here's a big one: are you actually talking to the right people? Your copy should feel like you're reading your ideal customer's mind.

5. Is your offer truly irresistible? Are you spelling out exactly why someone should care?

6. Have you sprinkled in some social proof? A few glowing testimonials can work wonders.

7. Lastly, how does it all look on mobile? More and more people are browsing on their phones these days.

You'd be amazed how often I'm asked to diagnose underperforming landing pages, and it frequently comes down to insufficient testing. Sometimes, businesses are even sending users to the wrong page entirely. It may sound obvious, but you should always test your entire sales funnel as if you were a potential customer. This simple step can uncover glaring issues you might have overlooked.

Systematic testing of your landing page can reveal exactly where you're losing potential leads.

Remember, refining is all about making incremental adjustments until you've crafted a page that converts effectively. Even small improvements can significantly boost your conversion rates.

6. What if they don't buy?

If people are clicking on your ads, opting into your enquiry or quote form or scheduling a call, and they still don't buy, we need to pinpoint why. Often, the culprit is slow response time. Imagine a potential client enquiring about your consulting services or requesting a quote for a home renovation – how quickly do you get back to them? In a world of instant gratification, delays can cost you business.

Many service providers fall into the trap of generating leads but failing to nurture them effectively – no confirmation email, no follow-up call, no additional information sent. It's a common scenario: you've invested in attracting interest, but then drop the ball when it comes to closing the deal. Not only are you letting those leads fall through the cracks, but you're missing out on huge revenue opportunities.

Your team's approach could also be the issue. Are your service representatives contacting leads promptly? Do they have the skills to effectively communicate the value of your services? This highlights the importance of both training and automation. There's no reason not to send immediate, personalised responses through your CRM system, even if it's just to acknowledge the enquiry and set expectations for next steps.

If leads consistently aren't converting into clients, it suggests a significant gap in your sales process. The solution lies in your data. Analyse your numbers carefully – they'll reveal where potential clients are dropping off. Are they not progressing past the initial consultation? Is your pricing structure turning them away? Are you failing to demonstrate the unique value of your services? The data will tell you where the problem is, then you can fix it.

Plugging the holes in your sales process is all about identifying drop off points and 'leaks', and refining your sales funnel to increase the performance of every link in the chain, one by one. By addressing these issues, you can refine your approach and turn more of those hard-won leads into loyal clients for your service business.

Optimising your metrics for maximum ROI

For service businesses looking to scale with digital advertising campaigns, understanding some key campaign performance metrics is crucial.

AD (FACEBOOK)

COST PER CLICK?
CLICK-THROUGH RATE?

CPC and CTR

There are two key metrics that can make or break your digital advertising efforts: cost per click (CPC) and click-through rate (CTR). You'll find these in your ad platform's analytics. If you're dipping your toes into online ads, you'll want to watch these metrics closely. They'll tell you whether your ads are hitting the mark or falling flat (and thus losing money); if it's the latter, you'll need to refine them. Here's how they work.

CTR is the percentage of people who click your ad after seeing it. For example, if 1,000 people see your ad and ten of them click on it, your CTR is 1%:

Clicks / Impressions = Click-Through Rate
10 / 1,000 = 1%

CPC is determined by the ad platform's auction model. You can calculate it by dividing your ad spend by the number of clicks:

Spend / Clicks = Cost Per Click
$1,000 / 10 clicks = $100 per click

For service businesses, a high CPC or low CTR suggests your ad isn't resonating with your target audience. Perhaps your plumbing service ad isn't highlighting the right pain points, or your consulting firm's value proposition isn't clear.

The average CPC for service-based businesses can vary quite a bit depending on the industry, location, and competition. But as of this writing, here's a general breakdown of industry benchmarks, so you can get an idea of where your CPC sits:

- Local services (eg, plumbers, electricians, home repair)
  - Typical CPC: $3 to $10
  - In more competitive markets, it's not unusual for CPCs to go beyond $10

- Legal services (eg, attorneys, law firms)
  - Typical CPC: $5 to $25
  - For highly competitive areas like personal injury law, CPCs can easily climb to $50 plus
- Healthcare services (eg, dentists, chiropractors)
  - Typical CPC: $2 to $10
  - Specialised healthcare services, such as cosmetic surgery or fertility clinics, tend to push towards the higher end
- Financial services (eg, accountants, financial advisers)
  - Typical CPC: $3 to $20
  - Certain high-demand niches like insurance or loan services can see CPCs soaring to $50 or more
- Real estate services (eg, realtors, property management)
  - Typical CPC: $1 to $10
  - Markets dealing with luxury properties or prime real estate tend to see higher CPCs
- Education services (eg, tutoring, specialised schools)
  - Typical CPC: $1 to $6

- Specialised programmes or certifications can increase this range

Ultimately, your CPC will depend on the platform you're using, your bidding strategy and how competitive your specific market is.

Conversion rate (CR) and cost per lead (CPL)

Two more crucial numbers for your digital marketing are your CR and your CPL. These metrics are the next step in understanding how well your online efforts are paying off.

Your CR is all about how many of the clicks on your ad turn into actual leads. Here's how you calculate it:

Leads / Clicks = Conversion Rate
1 / 10 = 10%

Your CPL tells you how much you're spending to get each lead. If you spend $100 and get 10 leads, each lead costs you $10:

Budget Spent / Leads = Cost Per Lead
$100 / 10 leads = $10 per lead

Now, what's a good or bad number here? That's where it gets tricky. It really depends on your business, and your CLV. The higher your CLV, the more you can afford to spend to acquire a client.

If you're a consultant charging $2,000 per project, spending $10 per lead is a steal. Even if you only land one client out of 200 leads, you're still in the black. For a solar panel installation business charging $15,000 per job, you might be happy to spend thousands on leads. If 10 out of 100 leads become customers, that's $150,000 in revenue – not too shabby! But if you're selling a $9.99 online course, a $7.50 CPL is going to hurt your wallet pretty quickly.

Marketing for lower-ticket items is a whole different game, demanding a unique approach. With slim margins, you need laser-focused targeting and a super-efficient funnel. It's about balancing volume with cost-effective strategies like automation, upselling and smart email marketing. The aim? Create a lean marketing machine that turns a profit despite lower price points. It's tricky, but doable with the right tactics.

Keeping an eye on these numbers is crucial for fine-tuning your marketing. They'll tell you if you're turning clicks into leads in a way that actually makes financial sense for your business. If the numbers aren't adding up, it's time to make some changes – and fast!

Sales Conversion Rate (SCR) and Cost Per Sale (CPS)

Tracking sales revenue can be easier for e-commerce businesses, because of the immediate, real-time nature of the sales process. But those with longer sales cycles, such as service businesses, still need to monitor the right metrics to refine their marketing efforts.

One crucial number for all businesses is the sales conversion rate (SCR), which measures the percentage of leads that result in actual sales. For instance, if you make 10 sales from 100 leads, your SCR is 10%. It's as simple as that.

Sales / Leads = Sales Conversion Rate
10 / 100 = 10%

We also need to establish how much it costs to acquire each customer (not a lead, an actual paying customer). In an automated, digital marketing system like mine, the exact figure is easy to calculate. For example, if an ad budget of $1,000 generates one sale, the cost per sale is $1,000. Ten sales, it's $100, and so on.

Budget / Sales = Cost Per Sale
$1,000 / 1 sale = $1,000

What's a good number here? Again, it depends on your business, and again, you need to factor in CLV. A solar panel installer might be happy with a $1,000 cost per sale on a $15,000 job. But for a $20 monthly boiler care plan, that same cost would be a disaster. Sometimes, you might lose money upfront but make it back in the long-term through repeat business or upsells. It's all about making sure the numbers add up for your specific business model.

If your costs are too high, you might need to tweak your targeting, change your offer, or even rethink your whole sales funnel. The key, as we keep learning in this chapter, is to keep testing and optimising until you find what works for your business.

Split and A/B testing: Find what works best

Split testing, or A/B testing, is standard practice in digital marketing. It's a practical method for ad optimisation that helps improve performance. Here's how it works:

You create two versions of an ad, identical except for one element. This could be the headline, image or CTA. Both ads are then shown to similar audiences, and you measure which performs better.

Facebook makes A/B testing particularly straightforward. You can set up tests directly from the Ad Manager, either by using the built-in A/B test feature or by manually creating duplicate ads or campaigns with variations. This flexibility allows you to test everything from ad creative to audience targeting.

Let's consider an example for a plumbing service:

Version A headline: 'Twenty-four-seven emergency plumbing services'

Version B headline: 'Leaky pipe? We'll fix it in 60 minutes or less'

Everything else in the ad remains the same. You might run these two versions simultaneously for a week and compare their performance. Facebook's Ad Manager provides clear metrics to track your results. You can easily see which ad performs better in terms of clicks, conversions or any other metric you're targeting. Once you've identified a winner – let's say Version B generates 30% more clicks – you can use this as the foundation for your next test.

This is where the iterative nature of A/B testing comes into play. You might now test different images with the winning headline, or try variations of the CTA button. Each test builds on the insights from the previous one, gradually refining your ad for optimal performance. You might test headlines one week, images the next and then move on to audience targeting or ad placement. This constant optimisation is key to maintaining and improving ad performance over time.

While there is a cost associated with testing, it's generally a worthwhile investment, as the insights gained are extremely valuable. By incorporating A/B testing into your marketing strategy, you're taking a methodical, data-driven approach to optimisation. It's a reliable way to refine your campaigns and potentially improve your marketing ROI.

A never-ending journey

Whether you're tweaking ad creative, refining your landing page copy or adjusting your ad budget, the process of optimisation is ongoing. It's this commitment to constant refinement that can give you an edge in your digital marketing efforts and separates thriving from stagnating businesses.

ACCELERATOR 9: REFINE

Please don't worry – this is all part and parcel of digital marketing. Refining your messaging, and your automated marketing system overall, isn't a sign of failure; it's a normal, necessary step in creating a high-converting funnel. Keep testing, keep refining and you'll get there.

Refining your automated marketing system means continually improving its effectiveness. Success comes from being agile and responsive, maintaining a mindset of continuous improvement, using data to inform your decisions and making incremental changes that lead to better results over time.

As we wrap up the RED Method, it's crucial to recognise that this journey of optimisation is not a one-off task but a fundamental shift in how you drive your marketing efforts. The RED Method has provided you with a powerful, high-performance foundation, turning your business into a predictable Leads Machine. But it's your commitment to ongoing refinement that will fuel sustained success.

The digital landscape is evolving at breakneck speed, and your competitors are constantly revving their engines. But equipped with these insights, you're not just keeping pace; you're positioning yourself as a market leader. With the RED Method blueprint in hand, you have what it takes to become the go-to choice, the business that customers think of first and trust implicitly.

So, what's your next move? Will you take that vital first step towards transforming your business? Just like any long journey, the road to consistent, predictable growth begins with a single action.

In the final chapter, we'll explore what this future could look like for your business and how to maintain momentum as you implement the RED Method. The best part? Your success story is just waiting to hit the road. Let's turn the page and start that new chapter.

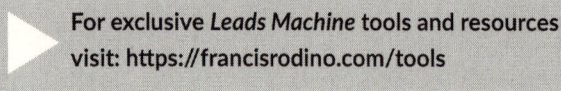

> For exclusive *Leads Machine* **tools and resources visit: https://francisrodino.com/tools**

Conclusion: Your Business Future – Drift Or Decide

The path to consistent, predictable sales should now be clear. You're standing at the threshold of a transformative journey for your business. With the RED Method as your guide, you're equipped with powerful tools and strategies to revolutionise your marketing approach.

Imagine waking up each morning to a steady stream of qualified leads, your calendar filled with sales calls, and your business thriving like never before. This isn't just a pipe dream – it's the reality that awaits when you implement these strategies.

You've learned how to craft a compelling strategy, build an automated system that works tirelessly on your behalf and scale and refine your efforts to reach new heights. Now it's time to turn that knowledge into action. Every day you delay is a day of potential growth lost.

So let's cut to the chase and look at how your current circumstances might play out over time, particularly in the context of the model we've just walked through – the RED Method (Roadmap, Engine, Drive).

Where do you see your company now? More importantly, where do you want to see it in the future?

The RED Method isn't just a set of theoretical concepts. It's a model for transforming your service business into a lean, mean, client-attracting machine. But here's a truth bomb: knowledge without action is like having a winning lottery ticket you never cash in.

If we look at your current reality, we can predict that with the simple passing of time – whether it's twelve months, twenty-four months, thirty-six months, whatever – you will end up in one of four future circumstances. The question is: which one?

1. **Winning:** You're at the pinnacle, the cream of the crop. Your automated sales funnel is humming along like a well-oiled machine, bringing in a steady stream of high-quality leads. You're not just competing; you're dominating. Your brand is synonymous with excellence in your industry. Clients aren't just choosing you; they're clamouring to work with you.

2. **Competing:** You're in the game, holding your own. You've implemented some of the strategies we've discussed, and you're seeing results. You're not quite at the top of the mountain,

but you're climbing steadily. Your business is growing, but there's still untapped potential.

3. **Playing:** You're in the race, but you're not setting the pace. You're doing OK, maybe even turning a profit, but you're constantly playing catch-up. You're reactive rather than proactive, always one step behind the market leaders.

4. **Exhausting:** This is the danger zone. You're working harder than ever, but it feels like you're running on a treadmill – lots of effort, no forward motion. Your competitors are leaving you in the dust, and you're starting to question why you got into business in the first place.

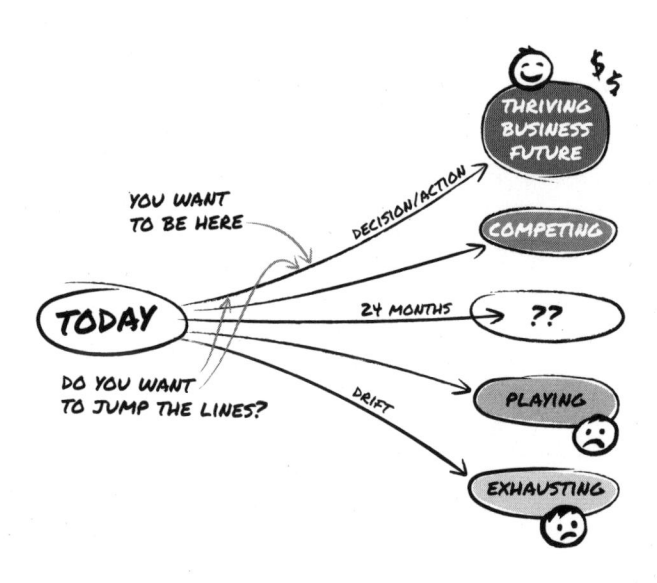

LEADS MACHINE

Here's the thing about business growth. The path from where you are today to where you want to be, isn't a straight line. It's a steep curve upwards, and gravity is always pulling you down.

If you do nothing, if you let yourself drift, there's only one direction you're heading – down to that exhausting zone. It might take a year, it might take three, but make no mistake, drift always goes down. It's like trying to paddle upstream in a leaky canoe – the moment you stop paddling, you start losing ground. Even if you're participating, making some effort but not fully committed, you're still on a downward trajectory. It's just not as steep of a free-fall.

The curve up to competing is where things start to get interesting. You're making progress, you're seeing results, but it's incremental. You're climbing, but it's a steady ascent rather than a rocket launch.

But that winning curve? That's where the magic happens. That's where success builds on success, where your efforts compound and your business takes off like a rocket. The difference between the exhausting zone and the winning zone isn't luck or circumstances – it's decision and action. And to get on it, you need to take action and do smart things.

So let me ask you this: which line are you on right now?

If you're like most of the service business owners I've worked with, you're probably somewhere around the participating zone. And here's the thing – the gap between where you are and that winning line? It's never going to be smaller than it is right now.

CONCLUSION: YOUR BUSINESS FUTURE – DRIFT OR DECIDE

Every day you wait, every day you put off implementing the RED Method, that gap grows. The market doesn't stand still. Your competitors aren't twiddling their thumbs. They're out there, right now, fighting for the same clients *you* want. The first decision you need to make is this: are you going to jump lines? Are you going to commit to putting yourself on that winning trajectory?

The RED Method is a proven framework that can put you on that upward curve, that can help you build momentum and compound your successes.

Once you're on that winning line, the second decision is this: are you going to ride the curve? Are you going to consistently apply these strategies, refine your approach and push yourself to reach the highest levels of success?

The final question to ask yourself is: how long are you prepared to wait before you take positive, structured action? How many more months or years are you willing to let slip by before you commit to a blueprint that can get you to where you want to be?

In the world of business, the spoils don't go to the hesitant. They go to the bold, to the decisive, to those who are willing to take action when others are still pondering their options.

So what's it going to be? Are you ready to transform your service business into a client-attracting powerhouse? Are you ready to leave the exhausting hamster wheel behind and step into the winner's circle? Can you picture a future where your sales flow as steadily and predictably as the tides, securing not just your business, but your family's wellbeing for the next decade or two?

The question isn't whether you can afford to take this leap – it's whether you can afford not to.

How long are you prepared to wait?

> ▶ **For exclusive *Leads Machine* tools and resources visit: https://francisrodino.com/tools**

Acknowledgements

This book is the result of countless experiences and interactions, and I'm deeply grateful to everyone who has been part of this journey.

To my wife, Carolina, thank you for your unwavering support through every triumph and setback. Your belief in me has been my greatest strength.

To my daughter, Leia, you are my inspiration. You opened me up to a kind of love I never thought possible. And in this digital, virtual world, your smile brings me back to reality.

To my parents, thank you for being there, even if you may not understand. Your support and love has guided me through life.

I'm indebted to my mentors: John Logar, Daniel Priestley, Simon Bowen and Greg Scharnagl. Your insights and guidance have been instrumental in shaping my approach to business and life.

The Author

Francis Rodino is a renowned expert in sales automation and digital marketing with a career spanning over two decades. As a High Level SaaSpreneur award winner, he has established himself as a leader in demand generation, helping businesses worldwide stand out in a crowded digital landscape.

Known for his expertise in creating demand for products and services, Francis has led global digital media teams as Global Head of Digital for a $3 billion data analytics company, directing campaigns that engaged millions and transformed brand visibility. His achievements include launching NatWest's first online banking platform and spearheading campaigns for PlayStation, Disney and the Olympics, as well as helping Top Gear reach 10 million Facebook followers.

Originally from New York City, Francis's journey through Italy and the UK led him to blend creativity with data-driven strategy, a distinctive approach he brings to his companies, Lead Hero AI and Clinic Convert. Specialising in AI-driven marketing, he enables SMEs to automate lead generation and conversion, freeing business owners to focus on core operations while his systems nurture high-quality leads.

As an international speaker and consultant, Francis shares his expertise through workshops, seminars and direct consultancy, offering actionable strategies for sustainable growth. His proprietary RED Method, the core of *Leads Machine*, guides business owners in building reliable, automated lead-generation engines.

Through his consultancy, workshops and book, Francis is committed to helping businesses not only adapt to the demands of digital marketing but excel, creating sustainable demand and achieving their growth potential.

🌐 francisrodino.com